# 5-INGREDIENTS
# MEXICAN
## CUISINES

**GARDEN** *of* **GRAPES.**




First Edition: 2023

Published by Garden of Grapes.

Printed in USA

The recipes, techniques, and tips in this cookbook are intended for personal use only. The author and publisher are not responsible for any adverse effects or consequences resulting from the use of the recipes or suggestions in this book.

Library of Congress Cataloging-in-Publication Data:

First edition.
Includes index.

Manufactured in USA

# Introduction

Ladies and gentlemen, fellow aficionados of authentic Mexican cuisine,

A warm and hearty welcome to you all as we embark on a culinary journey through the pages of "Mexican Fiesta with 5 Ingredients." You've opened the door to a world of simple, satisfying, and soul-warming Mexican dishes, crafted with love and a dash of fiesta spirit.

You might wonder, "Why a cookbook with just 5 ingredients?" It's a fair question, and the answer is simple – to bring the joy of Mexican cooking into your life without overwhelming your kitchen. Inspired by the vibrant and diverse flavors of Mexico, I wanted to create a cookbook that captures the essence of this remarkable cuisine while keeping it accessible to every home chef.

As we traverse this delightful journey, you can expect to uncover a treasure trove of over 100 uncomplicated yet mouthwatering recipes, each thoughtfully designed to encapsulate the true spirit of Mexico. This isn't about spending hours in the kitchen or hunting for elusive ingredients; it's about savoring the bold, authentic flavors of Mexico without the fuss.

You'll find dishes that span the rich tapestry of Mexican cuisine, from street food favorites to beloved family recipes passed down through generations. Tacos, enchiladas, salsas, and a variety of other delectable surprises await your eager palate.

While the focus may be on simplicity, don't think for a moment that we've sacrificed authenticity. These recipes have been fine-tuned to retain their genuine Mexican character, ensuring that every bite transports you to the bustling markets and vibrant streets of Mexico.

So, prepare to unleash your inner chef, don your sombrero, and let the fiesta begin! You're about to embark on a culinary voyage filled with flavor, culture, and the joy of sharing a delicious meal with loved ones.

I am humbled and thrilled to be your culinary guide on this adventure. Let's celebrate the joy of Mexican cooking with just 5 ingredients, shall we?

Bienvenidos y buen provecho (Welcome and enjoy your meal)!

Garden of Grapes

# Cooking Philosophy or Approach

Hey there, fellow culinary thrill-seekers!

As we dive into the heart of this fiesta, I want you to know what makes "Mexican Fiesta with 5 Ingredients" tick. You see, every cookbook has a philosophy, a culinary approach, and a soul that defines it. This cookbook, our cookbook, is all about one simple principle: the joy of 5-ingredient Mexican dishes. We're on a quest to make sure that you can whip up the authentic flavors of Mexico with ease and without a crazy-long shopping list.

Our approach to cooking is like the beating heart of a mariachi band – full of life, flavor, and passion. We embrace simplicity, we cherish bold, vibrant flavors, and we honor the deep roots of Mexican cuisine. It's like taking the very essence of Mexico and bringing it to your kitchen, using just five key ingredients. That's right, we're keeping it simple without sacrificing that delicious fiesta of tastes that Mexican food is famous for.

Now, let me give you a sneak peek at some of the techniques and ingredients that light up the pages of this cookbook. It's all about the classics – sizzling fajitas, zesty tacos, mouthwatering enchiladas, and yes, of course, those creamy guacamoles. We'll walk you through techniques that have been passed down through generations. Think about it as a culinary journey, where you get to explore and celebrate the rich tapestry of Mexican cuisine with just five ingredients in your shopping cart.

Our secret sauce? Well, that's for you to discover as you flip through the pages and embark on your own Mexican culinary adventure. You'll find the magic in the pairing of ingredients, the balance of flavors, and the sheer joy of sharing a meal that speaks to the soul. And with pictures included, you'll have a visual fiesta right at your fingertips.

So, whether you're an experienced chef or just starting on your culinary voyage, this cookbook is your passport to authentic Mexican flavors made simple. It's about celebrating the joy of good food, good company, and the unmistakable spirit of Mexico. We can't wait for you to join us on this flavorful ride.

Grab your apron, your sombrero, and let's cook up a storm! ¡Vámonos! 🌮🌶️🇲🇽

Yours in Mexican culinary revelry,
Garden of Grapes

**Beef Tacos**
See page, 24

# Tips for Successful Cooking

Ladies and gentlemen, hungry souls and culinary explorers,

As we part ways on this gastronomic journey through the vibrant and flavorful world of Mexican cuisine, I want to ensure you're well-equipped to continue your adventure at home. In "Mexican Fiesta with 5 Ingredients," we've aimed to simplify the art of Mexican cooking, bringing you the joy of creating over 100 simple and satisfying dishes with minimal fuss. But before you don your apron and dive into the delicious world of Mexican flavors, let's arm you with some invaluable tips for successful cooking.

**1. Freshness is Key:** Mexican cuisine is all about fresh, vibrant ingredients. When selecting your produce, look for bright colors, firm textures, and, most importantly, that mouthwatering aroma. Freshness is your passport to an authentic Mexican experience.

**2. Spice It Up (or Down):** Mexican cuisine can be as fiery as you like, but remember that chiles vary in heat. To control the spice level, remove the seeds and inner membranes for milder dishes, and keep them for a fiery fiesta.

**3. Salsa Secrets:** A great salsa can elevate any dish. Experiment with different salsas, from the smoky richness of chipotle to the fresh tang of pico de gallo. Adjust the level of spiciness to suit your taste.

**4. Tortilla Tips:** Corn or flour, you decide. For the perfect tortilla, heat them briefly on a dry skillet or comal. That warm, slightly charred tortilla aroma? It's the siren song of Mexican cooking.

**5. Slow and Low:** Many Mexican dishes require patience. Whether it's simmering a rich mole sauce or slow-cooking tender meat for tacos, take your time. Let those flavors meld and mingle.

**6. The Avocado Dilemma:** The ripeness of avocados can be your biggest challenge. If they're too firm, place them in a paper bag for a day or two to speed up the ripening process. If they're too soft, well, it's time for guacamole.

**7. Cheese Choices:** Mexican cheese is a universe unto itself. Cotija for crumbly, queso fresco for fresh, and Oaxaca for melting. Don't be shy about exploring these delicious dairy delights.

**8. The Art of Tamales:** If you're diving into the world of tamales, remember that making them is a labor of love. It's a tradition as much as a recipe. Get the whole family involved and make a tamalada out of it.

**9. Meat Matters:** Marinate, season, and slow-cook your meats. Whether it's carnitas, barbacoa, or pollo asado, take the time to infuse those flavors.

**10. Margarita Magic:** No Mexican feast is complete without a margarita. Salted rim or not, that's your choice. But make it with quality tequila and freshly squeezed lime juice.

Now, you're armed with the knowledge, the recipes, and the passion. It's time to embark on your Mexican culinary adventure. Enjoy the journey, and remember, while cooking may require a bit of skill, it's the heart and soul you put into it that truly matters.

Buen provecho, my friends! May your Mexican fiesta be a joyous one.

Yours in flavor and adventure,
Garden of Grapes

# Kitchen Essentials

Hey there, my fellow amigos of flavor,

Before we part ways, I wanted to give you a little gift to keep the Mexican fiesta alive in your kitchen. Below, you'll find a list of kitchen essentials that have been our trusty sidekicks throughout our culinary journey. These are the amigos you can rely on to whip up those 5-ingredient Mexican delights with ease.

**Kitchen Essentials:**

**1. Chef's Knife:** Your trusty comrade in slicing, dicing, and chopping. It's the sword of the culinary world, and every Mexican dish begins with a well-handled blade.

**2. Cutting Board:** This is where the magic happens. Go for a spacious, durable board – you'll thank us when you're prepping mountains of fresh ingredients for your salsas and guacamole.

**3. Blender/Food Processor:** A blender or food processor is the heart of your Mexican fiesta. It'll turn your tomatoes, chilies, and other fresh ingredients into the perfect salsa or sauce, all in a matter of seconds.

**4. Molcajete and Tejolote:** For the authentic touch, a molcajete (mortar and pestle) is perfect for grinding spices and making salsas. It's not just a tool; it's a piece of Mexican culture.

**5. Cast Iron Skillet or Comal:** This will be your go-to for heating tortillas, toasting spices, and creating the perfect sear on your protein. It's your direct ticket to that smoky flavor that defines Mexican cuisine.

**6. Citrus Juicer:** Freshly squeezed lime or lemon juice is the zesty lifeblood of Mexican dishes. A citrus juicer makes it a breeze to extract every precious drop.

**Tips on How to Use These Tools Effectively:**

- When using your chef's knife, make sure it's sharp. A dull knife can be more dangerous than a sharp one. Keep it honed and ready for action.

- For your cutting board, keep one designated for fruits and veggies and another for proteins to prevent cross-contamination.

- When blending in your blender or food processor, start with the liquid ingredients at the bottom and gradually add the solids. This ensures a smooth and consistent blend.

- Your molcajete needs some seasoning before use. Grind some raw rice in it first to get rid of any lingering stone particles, then give it a thorough wash.

- Season your cast iron skillet regularly. This keeps it non-stick and prevents rust.

- When using your citrus juicer, roll your limes or lemons on the countertop before juicing. This breaks down the pulp and makes it easier to squeeze.

With these trusty sidekicks and a few useful tips, you're armed and ready to conquer the world of 5-ingredient Mexican cuisine. So, go forth, whip up those dishes with love, and let the fiesta continue in your very own kitchen.

Stay spicy and savor every bite, my friends. Until we meet again.

With the deepest appreciation,
Garden of Grapes

**Tostadas**
See page, 23

# Flavor Pairing Suggestions

Alright, my friends,

You've just embarked on a culinary adventure through the vibrant world of Mexican cuisine with our cookbook, "Mexican Fiesta with 5 Ingredients." You've tasted the bold, spicy, and soul-warming flavors of Mexico, all with just a handful of ingredients. But, what's an adventure without a bit of experimentation and creating something uniquely yours?

That's where our Flavor Pairing Suggestions come into play. We're all about turning your kitchen into a canvas, and you, the artist, wielding the brush. In this section, we give you a glimpse into the art of complementary flavors. Think of it as your flavor palette. Here's where you can let your creativity shine.

Mexican cuisine is rich and diverse, and experimenting with flavors is key to making it your own. Maybe you've fallen in love with the zesty tang of salsa, the creaminess of avocados, or the fiery kiss of jalapeños. Now, we invite you to play matchmaker with ingredients. Here are some ideas to inspire your culinary creativity:

**1. Citrus Zest and Fresh Herbs:** Elevate your dishes with the zing of citrus zest like lime or orange, paired with fresh herbs like cilantro or mint. Try a zesty lime cilantro rice or orange-infused guacamole for a refreshing twist.

**2. Creamy Avocado and Smoky Spices:** Avocado and smoky flavors like cumin or smoked paprika make a power couple. Blend them for a creamy, smoky guacamole or spice up your avocado toast.

**3. Sweet and Spicy:** Balance the heat of jalapeños or chipotle with a hint of sweetness. Try chipotle-honey-glazed grilled chicken or jalapeño-mango salsa for a sweet and fiery combo.

**4. Tropical Fruits and Heat:** Pineapple, mango, or coconut can add a touch of the tropics to your Mexican dishes. Combine them with spicy chiles for a delightful sweet-heat contrast.

**5. Rich Chocolate and Chile:** Chocolate and chiles are a classic Mexican duo. Experiment with a cocoa-chile rub for your meats or add a touch of chocolate to your mole sauce.

**6. Pickled Red Onions and Everything:**
Pickled red onions can add a punch of tangy, vibrant flavor to almost any Mexican dish. Tacos, nachos, and even grilled meats become culinary masterpieces with a few of these.

So there you have it, a canvas of flavors ready for your artistic touch. You've mastered the basics with our 5-ingredient recipes, and now it's time to let your creativity run wild. Feel free to combine, experiment, and find your own perfect flavor pairings.

Remember, Mexican cuisine is all about passion, and it's as much about the journey as it is about the destination. We can't wait to see what mouthwatering creations you come up with. Feel free to share your discoveries and inspire other fellow adventurers in the world of "Mexican Fiesta with 5 Ingredients."

To your culinary masterpieces and flavorful discoveries,
Garden of Grapes

**Tinga Tacos**
See page, 33

# Table of contents

# Chapter 1:
## Appetizing Starters

**4**
servings

**150**
calories
per
serving

**15**
minutes

# Guacamole with Tortilla Chips

Dive into the flavors of Mexico with this creamy Guacamole! A classic dip made with ripe avocados and zesty lime juice, perfect for sharing at any gathering.

## Ingredients:

- 4 ripe avocados
- 1 small red onion, finely diced
- 2 cloves of garlic, minced
- 2 tomatoes, diced
- 1/4 cup fresh cilantro, chopped
- Juice of 2 limes
- Salt and pepper to taste

## Directions

1. Cut the avocados in half, remove the pit, and scoop the flesh into a bowl.
2. Mash the avocado with a fork, leaving some chunks for texture.
3. Add the onion, garlic, tomatoes, cilantro, lime juice, salt, and pepper.
4. Mix well and adjust seasoning to taste.
5. Serve with tortilla chips for dipping.

Pro tip: To keep guacamole from turning brown, press plastic wrap directly onto the surface before refrigerating.

## Fun Facts

Did you know? Avocados are packed with healthy fats and are a good source of potassium and fiber. Guacamole is not just delicious; it's nutritious too!

6
servings

250
calories
per
serving

20
minutes

# Queso Fundido

Queso Fundido, a crowd-pleasing Mexican cheese dip, is perfect for cheese lovers. Melted cheese with chorizo and chiles served bubbling hot – a taste of pure indulgence.

## Ingredients:

- 1/2 pound chorizo sausage, casing removed
- 1/2 cup diced onions
- 1/2 cup diced red bell pepper
- 2 cups shredded Oaxaca cheese (or mozzarella)
- 1/4 cup chopped fresh cilantro
- Tortilla chips for dipping

## Directions

1. In a skillet, cook chorizo over medium heat until browned, breaking it into crumbles.
2. Add onions and bell pepper; sauté until softened.
3. Preheat oven to 350°F (175°C).
4. Transfer chorizo mixture to a baking dish.
5. Top with cheese and bake until bubbly and golden.
6. Garnish with cilantro and serve with tortilla chips.

Pro tip: Use a cast-iron skillet for a rustic presentation.

## Fun Facts

The name "Queso Fundido" translates to "melted cheese," and that's exactly what you'll get – a gooey, cheesy delight that disappears fast!

8 servings

20 calories per serving

10 minutes

# Salsa Fresca

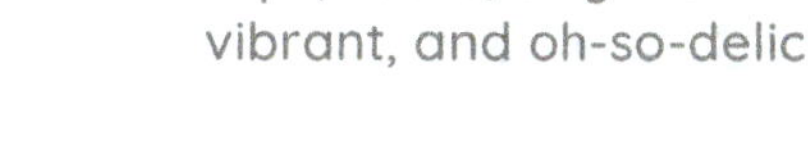


Salsa Fresca, a fresh tomato salsa, is a zesty burst of flavors. It's the perfect partner for tortilla chips, tacos, or grilled meats. Simple, vibrant, and oh-so-delicious!

## Ingredients:

- 4 ripe tomatoes, diced
- 1/2 cup diced red onion
- 1/4 cup chopped fresh cilantro
- 1 jalapeño, seeded and minced (adjust for heat)
- Juice of 2 limes
- Salt and pepper to taste

## Directions

1. Combine tomatoes, red onion, cilantro, and jalapeño in a bowl.
2. Squeeze lime juice over the mixture.
3. Season with salt and pepper.
4. Mix well and refrigerate for at least 30 minutes to let the flavors meld.
5. Serve with your favorite dishes or as a dip.

## Fun Facts

Did you know? Salsa Fresca is also known as "pico de gallo" or "fresh salsa" and is a staple in Mexican cuisine for its freshness and bright flavors.

12
poppers

80
calories
per
serving

30
minutes

# Jalapeño Poppers

Spice up your appetizer game with these Jalapeño Poppers! Creamy cheese and crispy bacon make for a fiery and flavorful treat that disappears as soon as they're served.

## Ingredients:

- 6 large jalapeño peppers, halved lengthwise and seeded
- 8 ounces cream cheese, softened
- 1 cup shredded cheddar cheese
- 12 slices bacon, cut in half
- Toothpicks

## Directions

1. In a bowl, mix cream cheese and cheddar cheese until well combined.
2. Fill each jalapeño half with the cheese mixture.
3. Wrap with bacon and secure with a toothpick.
4. Preheat oven to 375°F (190°C).
5. Bake poppers for 20-25 minutes until bacon is crispy and cheese is bubbly.
6. Serve hot and watch them disappear!

Pro tip: Wear gloves when handling jalapeños to avoid chili burn.

## Fun Facts

Did you know? The heat in jalapeños comes from a compound called capsaicin, which can provide a fiery kick or a subtle heat, depending on the pepper.

**4**
servings

**200**
calories
per
serving

**25**
minutes

# Mexican Street Corn

Elote, or Mexican Street Corn, is a savory-sweet delight. Grilled corn smothered in mayo, cheese, and spices, this street food classic is a taste of Mexico's vibrant flavors.

## Ingredients:

- 4 ears of corn, husked
- 1/4 cup mayonnaise
- 1/2 cup crumbled cotija cheese
- 1 teaspoon chili powder
- 1 lime, cut into wedges
- Fresh cilantro, for garnish

## Directions

1. Grill the corn over medium-high heat until lightly charred.
2. Brush each ear with a generous amount of mayonnaise.
3. Roll in crumbled cotija cheese, sprinkle with chili powder.
4. Serve with lime wedges and garnish with cilantro.

Pro tip: Use Greek yogurt for a lighter mayo alternative.

## Fun Facts

A common sight on the streets of Mexico, Elote is a tasty and messy affair. Embrace the mess; it's part of the experience!

4
servings

150
calories
per
serving

30
minutes

# Ceviche

Ceviche, a zesty seafood dish, is a taste of coastal Mexico. Fresh fish or shrimp marinated in citrus juices, mixed with veggies, and a hint of spice - it's a refreshing sensation!

## Ingredients:

- 1 pound fresh white fish or shrimp, diced
- 1 cup fresh lime juice
- 1/2 cup diced red onion
- 1/2 cup diced cucumber
- 1/4 cup chopped fresh cilantro
- 1 jalapeño, seeded and minced
- Salt and pepper to taste

## Directions

1. In a bowl, combine fish or shrimp and lime juice.
2. Let it marinate in the refrigerator for 15-20 minutes until it turns opaque.
3. Add red onion, cucumber, cilantro, and jalapeño.
4. Season with salt and pepper.
5. Serve chilled as a refreshing appetizer.

Pro tip: You can customize the heat level by adjusting the jalapeño seeds.

## Fun Facts

Did you know? The acid from the citrus juice "cooks" the seafood in ceviche, making it safe to eat without traditional cooking methods.

**4**
servings

**350**
calories
per
serving

**20**
minutes

# Chorizo Quesadillas

Chorizo Quesadillas are a flavor-packed delight. Spicy chorizo, melted cheese, and crispy tortillas create a satisfying and indulgent appetizer or snack.

## Ingredients:

- 8 small flour tortillas
- 1/2 pound chorizo sausage, cooked and crumbled
- 1 cup shredded Monterey Jack cheese
- 1/2 cup diced bell peppers
- 1/4 cup chopped green onions

## Directions

1. Lay out 4 tortillas and divide chorizo, cheese, bell peppers, and green onions evenly among them.
2. Top with the remaining tortillas.
3. Heat a skillet over medium-high heat.
4. Cook quesadillas for 2-3 minutes on each side until cheese is melted and tortillas are crispy.
5. Cut into wedges and serve hot.

Pro tip: Serve with sour cream and salsa for extra flavor.

## Fun Facts

These quesadillas are like a fiesta in your mouth, with the bold flavors of chorizo and the creaminess of melted cheese dancing together.

16 peppers

40 calories per serving

25 minutes

# Stuffed Mini Peppers

Stuffed Mini Peppers are bite-sized bursts of flavor. These little gems are filled with a creamy cheese mixture and roasted to perfection - an irresistible appetizer!

## Ingredients:

- 16 mini sweet peppers, halved and seeded
- 8 ounces cream cheese, softened
- 1/2 cup shredded cheddar cheese
- 1/4 cup chopped fresh parsley
- Salt and pepper to taste

## Directions

1. Preheat the oven to 375°F (190°C).
2. Mix cream cheese, cheddar cheese, parsley, salt, and pepper in a bowl.
3. Fill each pepper half with the cheese mixture.
4. Arrange on a baking sheet and bake for 15-20 minutes until peppers are tender and cheese is golden.
5. Serve warm.

Pro tip: Add a pinch of smoked paprika for extra flavor.

## Fun Facts

These stuffed peppers are like bite-sized pieces of heaven, with a perfect balance of creamy and crunchy textures.

12
taquitos

180
calories
per
serving

35
minutes

# Taquitos

Taquitos, rolled tortillas filled with savory goodness, are a Mexican delight. Whether filled with chicken, beef, or veggies, they're crispy bites of pure joy!

## Ingredients:

- 12 small corn tortillas
- 2 cups cooked and shredded chicken or beef
- 1 cup shredded cheddar cheese
- 1/2 cup diced green chiles
- 1/4 cup diced onions
- 1 teaspoon cumin
- Oil for frying

## Directions

1. In a bowl, mix chicken or beef, cheddar cheese, green chiles, onions, and cumin.
2. Warm tortillas to make them pliable.
3. Place filling on each tortilla and roll tightly.
4. Heat oil in a skillet over medium-high heat.
5. Fry taquitos until golden and crispy.
6. Serve with salsa and sour cream.

Pro tip: Baking them is a healthier alternative to frying.

## Fun Facts

Taquitos are often served as a finger food at parties and gatherings, making them a crowd-pleaser.

4
servings

300
calories
per
serving

45
minutes

# Chiles Rellenos

Chiles Rellenos, stuffed poblano peppers with cheese, are a hearty and comforting dish. They're baked to golden perfection and smothered in a rich tomato sauce - a taste of Mexico's soul food.

## Ingredients:

- 4 large poblano peppers
- 1 cup shredded Monterey Jack cheese
- 1 cup shredded cheddar cheese
- 3 large eggs
- 1 cup all-purpose flour
- 2 cups tomato sauce
- 1/2 cup diced onions
- 2 cloves garlic, minced
- Oil for frying

## Directions

1. Roast poblano peppers over an open flame or broil until charred.
2. Place them in a plastic bag to steam, then peel off the skin.
3. Make a small slit in each pepper and remove seeds.
4. Stuff with a mixture of both cheeses.
5. In separate bowls, whisk eggs and place flour.
6. Dip each pepper in flour, then egg, and fry until golden.
7. In a separate pan, sauté onions and garlic, then add tomato sauce.
8. Simmer until heated through.
9. Pour the sauce over the stuffed peppers.
10. Bake until bubbly.

Pro tip: Serve with Mexican crema and cilantro for extra flavor.

## Fun Facts

Chiles Rellenos are a symbol of Mexican comfort food, with a rich history dating back to colonial times.

# Chapter 2:
## Sizzling Salsas & Dips

6
servings

15
calories
per
serving

20
minutes

# Salsa Verde

Salsa Verde, the "green sauce" of Mexico, is a tangy and slightly spicy delight. Made with tomatillos, it's perfect for drizzling over tacos, enchiladas, or grilled meats.

## Ingredients:

- 1 pound tomatillos, husked and rinsed
- 2 cloves garlic, peeled
- 1/2 cup diced onion
- 1/2 cup fresh cilantro leaves
- 1 jalapeño, seeded (adjust for heat)
- Juice of 1 lime
- Salt to taste

## Directions

1. Place tomatillos and garlic in a saucepan, cover with water, and bring to a boil.
2. Simmer for 5 minutes until tomatillos soften.
3. Drain and transfer to a blender.
4. Add onion, cilantro, jalapeño, lime juice, and salt.
5. Blend until smooth.
6. Serve chilled.

Pro tip: Roast the tomatillos for a smoky flavor variation.

## Fun Facts

Salsa Verde gets its vibrant green color from tomatillos, which are a staple in Mexican cuisine. They have a unique tartness that adds zing to the sauce.

8 servings

10 calories per serving

15 minutes

# Pico de Gallo

Pico de Gallo, a fresh tomato salsa, is the essence of simplicity. It's a medley of diced tomatoes, onions, cilantro, and jalapeños - a burst of garden-fresh flavors.

## Ingredients:

- 4 ripe tomatoes, diced
- 1/2 cup diced red onion
- 1/4 cup chopped fresh cilantro
- 1 jalapeño, seeded and minced (adjust for heat)
- Juice of 1 lime
- Salt and pepper to taste

## Directions

1. Combine tomatoes, red onion, cilantro, and jalapeño in a bowl.
2. Squeeze lime juice over the mixture.
3. Season with salt and pepper.
4. Mix well and refrigerate for at least 30 minutes to let the flavors meld.
5. Serve as a topping or dip.

Pro tip: Use fresh, ripe tomatoes for the best flavor.

## Fun Facts

Pico de Gallo, also known as "salsa fresca," is a classic condiment in Mexican cuisine. Its vibrant colors make it a feast for the eyes as well as the palate.

6
servings

45
calories
per
serving

15
minutes

# Mango Salsa

Mango Salsa is a sweet and spicy dance of flavors. Ripe mangoes, jalapeños, and lime juice create a tropical twist perfect for grilled chicken or fish.

## Ingredients:

- 2 ripe mangoes, diced
- 1/2 cup diced red onion
- 1/4 cup chopped fresh cilantro
- 1 jalapeño, seeded and minced (adjust for heat)
- Juice of 2 limes
- Salt and pepper to taste

## Directions

1. Combine mangoes, red onion, cilantro, and jalapeño in a bowl.
2. Squeeze lime juice over the mixture.
3. Season with salt and pepper.
4. Mix well and refrigerate for at least 30 minutes to let the flavors meld.
5. Serve with grilled proteins or as a snack with tortilla chips.

Pro tip: For extra heat, leave some jalapeño seeds.

## Fun Facts

Mango Salsa brings a taste of the tropics to your table, and the sweetness of mangoes balances the spice of jalapeños perfectly.

6
servings

25
calories
per
serving

25
minutes

# Salsa Roja

Salsa Roja, the "red sauce" of Mexico, is a rich and versatile tomato-based salsa. With a touch of heat and smokiness, it's an all-purpose condiment for your Mexican dishes.

## Ingredients:

- 4 ripe tomatoes, roasted
- 2 cloves garlic, roasted
- 1/2 cup diced onion, sautéed
- 2 dried guajillo chiles, soaked and seeded
- 1 dried ancho chile, soaked and seeded
- 1 chipotle pepper in adobo sauce
- 1 teaspoon cumin
- Salt to taste

## Directions

1. Roast tomatoes and garlic until slightly charred.
2. Sauté onions until translucent.
3. In a blender, combine tomatoes, garlic, sautéed onions, soaked chiles, chipotle pepper, cumin, and salt.
4. Blend until smooth.
5. Simmer in a saucepan for 10 minutes to meld flavors.
6. Serve warm or at room temperature.

Pro tip: Adjust the number of chiles for your preferred level of heat.

## Fun Facts

Salsa Roja is a versatile sauce used in various Mexican dishes, from enchiladas to tamales. Its smoky and slightly spicy flavor elevates any meal.

8 servings

60 calories per serving

10 minutes

# Chipotle Aioli

Chipotle Aioli is a creamy and smoky sauce with a hint of spice. Perfect for drizzling over grilled vegetables, sandwiches, or as a dip for sweet potato fries.

## Ingredients:

- 1 cup mayonnaise
- 2 cloves garlic, minced
- 2 tablespoons adobo sauce from canned chipotle peppers
- Juice of 1 lime
- Salt and pepper to taste

## Directions

1. In a bowl, whisk together mayonnaise, minced garlic, adobo sauce, and lime juice.
2. Season with salt and pepper to taste.
3. Refrigerate for 30 minutes to let the flavors meld.
4. Serve as a dipping sauce or drizzle over your favorite dishes.

Pro tip: Adjust the amount of adobo sauce for your preferred level of spiciness.

## Fun Facts

Chipotle Aioli adds a smoky and spicy kick to your meals, and it's a versatile condiment for sandwiches, burgers, and more.

8
servings

40
calories
per
serving

10
minutes

# Avocado Crema

Avocado Crema is a velvety, creamy sauce with a refreshing twist. It's the perfect companion for tacos, nachos, or as a salad dressing.

## Ingredients:

- 2 ripe avocados
- 1/2 cup sour cream
- Juice of 2 limes
- 1/4 cup chopped fresh cilantro
- Salt and pepper to taste

## Directions

1. Scoop the flesh of avocados into a blender.
2. Add sour cream, lime juice, cilantro, salt, and pepper.
3. Blend until smooth and creamy.
4. Adjust seasoning to taste.
5. Serve chilled.

Pro tip: If you prefer a thinner consistency, add a splash of water or more lime juice.

## Fun Facts

Avocado Crema combines the richness of avocados with the tang of lime and the creaminess of sour cream. It's a cool and creamy delight.

6 servings

20 calories per serving

20 minutes

# Charred Tomato Salsa

Charred Tomato Salsa is a smoky and robust dip. Fire-roasted tomatoes, chiles, and onions create a depth of flavor perfect for scooping with tortilla chips or topping grilled meats.

## Ingredients:

- 4 ripe tomatoes, charred
- 2 dried arbol chiles, soaked and seeded
- 1/2 cup diced onion, charred
- 2 cloves garlic, charred
- Juice of 1 lime
- Salt and pepper to taste

## Directions

1. Char tomatoes, chiles, onion, and garlic over an open flame or broil until slightly charred.
2. In a blender, combine charred ingredients, lime juice, salt, and pepper.
3. Blend until slightly chunky.
4. Serve at room temperature.

Pro tip: Adjust the number of chiles for your preferred level of heat.

## Fun Facts

Charred Tomato Salsa has a smoky, roasted flavor that adds depth to your dishes, making it a great accompaniment to grilled meats and more.

8
servings

120
calories
per
serving

15
minutes

# Queso Dip



Queso Dip is the ultimate cheesy indulgence. Melted cheese with a kick of green chiles - perfect for dipping tortilla chips or drizzling over nachos.

## Ingredients:

- 2 cups shredded cheddar cheese
- 1 cup shredded Monterey Jack cheese
- 1 cup diced green chiles (canned or fresh)
- 1 cup milk
- 2 tablespoons all-purpose flour
- 1/2 teaspoon cumin
- Salt and pepper to taste

## Directions

1. In a saucepan, whisk together milk and flour until smooth.
2. Add cheeses, green chiles, and cumin.
3. Cook over low heat, stirring until cheese is melted and the mixture is smooth.
4. Season with salt and pepper.
5. Serve hot as a dip or drizzle.

Pro tip: Add a dash of hot sauce for extra heat.

## Fun Facts

Queso Dip is a classic party favorite, and its creamy, cheesy goodness is hard to resist. Customize it with your favorite toppings like jalapeños or diced tomatoes.

**8**
servings

**50**
calories
per
serving

**5**
minutes

# Mexican Sour Cream

Mexican Sour Cream is a tangy and velvety condiment. It's the perfect complement to spicy dishes, tacos, or as a cooling dip for your favorite Mexican snacks.

## Ingredients:

- 1 cup sour cream
- Juice of 1 lime
- 1/4 cup chopped fresh cilantro
- Salt and pepper to taste

## Directions

1. In a bowl, whisk together sour cream, lime juice, cilantro, salt, and pepper.
2. Adjust seasoning to taste.
3. Serve chilled.

Pro tip: For extra zing, add a pinch of lime zest.

## Fun Facts

Mexican Sour Cream adds a tangy and cooling element to your Mexican dishes, balancing out the heat and spices. It's a must-have condiment.

8
servings

70
calories
per
serving

10
minutes

# Cilantro Lime Ranch Dip

Cilantro Lime Ranch Dip is a zesty twist on a classic. Creamy ranch with a burst of cilantro and lime - it's the perfect dip for veggies, chicken wings, or as a salad dressing.

## Ingredients:

- 1 cup mayonnaise
- 1/2 cup sour cream
- 1/4 cup chopped fresh cilantro
- Juice of 1 lime
- 1 packet ranch dressing mix
- Salt and pepper to taste

## Directions

1. In a bowl, combine mayonnaise, sour cream, cilantro, lime juice, and ranch dressing mix.
2. Mix until well combined.
3. Season with salt and pepper to taste.
4. Refrigerate for at least 30 minutes before serving.

Pro tip: Adjust the amount of cilantro and lime juice to suit your taste.

## Fun Facts

Cilantro Lime Ranch Dip adds a refreshing twist to the classic ranch. It's a versatile dip that pairs well with a variety of dishes.

# Chapter 3:
## Tasty Tacos & Tostadas

4
servings

300
calories
per
serving

30
minutes

# Beef Tacos

Beef Tacos are a classic favorite. Seasoned ground beef, fresh toppings, and warm tortillas come together in a delicious and satisfying meal.

## Ingredients:

- 1 pound ground beef
- 1 onion, diced
- 2 cloves garlic, minced
- 1 packet taco seasoning
- 1 cup shredded lettuce
- 1 cup diced tomatoes
- 1 cup shredded cheddar cheese
- 1/2 cup sour cream
- 8 small flour tortillas

## Directions

1. In a skillet, cook ground beef over medium-high heat until browned, breaking it into crumbles.
2. Add diced onions and garlic; sauté until onions are translucent.
3. Stir in taco seasoning and water (according to package directions) and simmer until thickened.
4. Warm tortillas in a dry skillet or microwave.
5. Spoon beef mixture onto each tortilla.
6. Top with lettuce, tomatoes, cheese, and sour cream.

Pro tip: Customize with your favorite toppings like jalapeños or guacamole.

## Fun Facts

Beef Tacos are a Tex-Mex classic, beloved for their savory and satisfying flavors. They're a crowd-pleaser at any gathering.

4
servings

250
calories
per
serving

30
minutes

# Chicken Tacos

Chicken Tacos are a tasty twist on the traditional beef. Seasoned chicken breast or thigh meat, paired with fresh toppings, makes for a flavorful taco experience.

## Ingredients:

- 1 pound boneless, skinless chicken breasts or thighs, sliced into strips
- 1 onion, diced
- 2 cloves garlic, minced
- 1 packet taco seasoning
- 1 cup shredded lettuce
- 1 cup diced tomatoes
- 1 cup shredded Monterey Jack cheese
- 1/2 cup salsa
- 8 small flour tortillas

## Directions

1. In a skillet, cook chicken strips over medium-high heat until cooked through.
2. Add diced onions and garlic; sauté until onions are translucent.
3. Stir in taco seasoning and water (according to package directions) and simmer until thickened.
4. Warm tortillas in a dry skillet or microwave.
5. Spoon chicken mixture onto each tortilla.
6. Top with lettuce, tomatoes, cheese, and salsa.

Pro tip: Marinate the chicken in lime juice and spices for extra flavor.

## Fun Facts

Chicken Tacos provide a leaner option with the same great taco taste. They're a healthier choice without sacrificing flavor.

**4 servings**

**280 calories per serving**

**30 minutes**

# Fish Tacos

Fish Tacos are a seafood delight. Crispy fish fillets, zesty slaw, and a drizzle of creamy sauce create a taco that's both crunchy and refreshing.

## Ingredients:

- 1 pound white fish fillets (such as cod or tilapia)
- 1 cup all-purpose flour
- 1 teaspoon paprika
- 1/2 teaspoon cayenne pepper
- 1 cup shredded cabbage or coleslaw mix
- 1/4 cup mayonnaise
- 1 tablespoon lime juice
- 8 small corn tortillas
- Oil for frying
- Salt and pepper to taste

## Fun Facts

Fish Tacos bring the flavors of the coast to your plate. The crispy fish and zesty slaw create a perfect balance of textures and tastes.

## Directions

1. In a bowl, combine flour, paprika, cayenne pepper, salt, and pepper.
2. Dredge fish fillets in the flour mixture, shaking off excess.
3. Heat oil in a skillet over medium-high heat.
4. Fry fish fillets until golden and crispy, about 3-4 minutes per side.
5. In another bowl, mix shredded cabbage, mayonnaise, and lime juice for slaw.
6. Warm corn tortillas in a dry skillet or microwave.
7. Place a fish fillet on each tortilla, top with slaw, and drizzle with sauce.

Pro tip: Use corn tortillas for an authentic touch.

4
servings

260
calories
per
serving

20
minutes

# Shrimp Tacos

Shrimp Tacos are a quick and flavorful option. Succulent shrimp, a burst of salsa, and a squeeze of lime make for a delightful taco experience.

## Ingredients:

- 1 pound large shrimp, peeled and deveined
- 1 tablespoon olive oil
- 1 teaspoon chili powder
- 1 teaspoon cumin
- 1 cup diced tomatoes
- 1/2 cup diced red onion
- 1/4 cup chopped fresh cilantro
- Juice of 2 limes
- 8 small corn tortillas
- Salt and pepper to taste

## Directions

1. In a bowl, toss shrimp with olive oil, chili powder, cumin, salt, and pepper.
2. Heat a skillet over medium-high heat and cook shrimp until pink and opaque, about 2-3 minutes per side.
3. In another bowl, combine diced tomatoes, red onion, cilantro, lime juice, salt, and pepper for salsa.
4. Warm corn tortillas in a dry skillet or microwave.
5. Place shrimp on each tortilla, top with salsa, and squeeze lime juice over the top.

Pro tip: Add sliced avocado or guacamole for extra creaminess.

## Fun Facts

Shrimp Tacos offer a taste of the sea with a burst of fresh flavors. They're a great choice for a quick and satisfying meal.

4
servings

200
calories
per
serving

25
minutes

# Veggie Tacos

Veggie Tacos are a flavorful meatless option. Roasted vegetables, black beans, and a sprinkle of cheese create a hearty and satisfying taco filling.

## Ingredients:

- 2 cups mixed bell peppers, sliced
- 1 cup red onion, sliced
- 1 cup zucchini, sliced
- 1 cup black beans, cooked
- 1 teaspoon chili powder
- 1/2 teaspoon cumin
- 1/2 cup shredded cheddar cheese
- 8 small flour tortillas
- Olive oil
- Salt and pepper to taste

## Directions

1. Preheat oven to 425°F (220°C).
2. Toss sliced vegetables with olive oil, chili powder, cumin, salt, and pepper.
3. Roast in the oven for 20-25 minutes until tender and slightly charred.
4. Warm flour tortillas in a dry skillet or microwave.
5. In a bowl, mix black beans with a pinch of salt.
6. Assemble tacos with roasted vegetables, black beans, and shredded cheese.

Pro tip: Top with avocado slices and a dollop of Greek yogurt or sour cream.

## Fun Facts

Veggie Tacos are a delicious and nutritious option, perfect for vegetarians and anyone looking to enjoy a meatless meal.

4
servings

320
calories
per
serving

25
minutes

# Tostadas

Tostadas are a crispy canvas for your favorite toppings. Crispy tortillas are piled high with beans, meat or veggies, and a colorful array of fresh toppings.

## Ingredients:

- 4 large corn tostada shells
- 1 cup refried beans
- 1 cup cooked and shredded chicken, beef, or beans for a vegetarian option
- 1 cup shredded lettuce
- 1 cup diced tomatoes
- 1/2 cup diced red onion
- 1/4 cup chopped fresh cilantro
- 1/2 cup crumbled queso fresco or shredded cheddar cheese
- 1/4 cup sour cream
- Salsa for drizzling
- Salt and pepper to taste

## Directions

1. Spread a layer of refried beans on each tostada shell.
2. Top with your choice of protein (chicken, beef, or beans).
3. Pile on shredded lettuce, diced tomatoes, red onion, cilantro, and cheese.
4. Drizzle with sour cream and salsa.
5. Season with salt and pepper.
6. Serve immediately.

Pro tip: Customize tostadas with your favorite toppings and sauces.

## Fun Facts

Tostadas are a versatile Mexican dish that allows you to get creative with your toppings. They're a crunchy delight with a burst of flavors.

4 servings

350 calories per serving

3 hours (includes slow cooking)

# Carnitas Tacos

Carnitas Tacos are all about tender, slow-cooked pork. The meat is cooked until it's melt-in-your-mouth tender, then crisped up for a delightful taco experience.

## Ingredients:

- 2 pounds pork shoulder, cut into chunks
- 1 onion, sliced
- 4 cloves garlic, minced
- 1 teaspoon cumin
- 1 teaspoon chili powder
- Juice of 2 oranges
- Juice of 1 lime
- Salt and pepper to taste
- 8 small corn tortillas
- Oil for frying

## Directions

1. In a slow cooker, combine pork chunks, sliced onions, minced garlic, cumin, chili powder, orange juice, lime juice, salt, and pepper.
2. Cook on low for 6-8 hours until pork is tender and easily shreds.
3. Remove pork from the slow cooker and shred.
4. Heat oil in a skillet over medium-high heat.
5. Add shredded pork and cook until crispy.
6. Warm corn tortillas in a dry skillet or microwave.
7. Assemble tacos with crispy carnitas and your favorite toppings.

Pro tip: Use the cooking juices for extra flavor and moisture.

## Fun Facts

Carnitas Tacos are a labor of love, with tender, slow-cooked pork that's crispy on the outside and succulent on the inside.

4
servings

320
calories
per
serving

30
minutes

# Carne Asada Tacos

Carne Asada Tacos feature marinated and grilled steak. The savory, tender beef pairs perfectly with fresh toppings and a squeeze of lime.

## Ingredients:

- 1 pound flank or skirt steak
- 1/4 cup orange juice
- Juice of 2 limes
- 4 cloves garlic, minced
- 1 teaspoon cumin
- 1 teaspoon chili powder
- 8 small corn tortillas
- 1 cup diced onions
- 1 cup chopped fresh cilantro
- Salsa for drizzling
- Salt and pepper to taste

## Directions

1. In a bowl, combine orange juice, lime juice, minced garlic, cumin, chili powder, salt, and pepper.
2. Marinate the steak in the mixture for at least 30 minutes, or overnight for better flavor.
3. Preheat a grill or grill pan over medium-high heat.
4. Grill the steak for 3-4 minutes per side for medium-rare, or to your desired doneness.
5. Remove from the grill and let it rest for a few minutes before slicing.
6. Warm corn tortillas in a dry skillet or microwave.
7. Assemble tacos with sliced carne asada, diced onions, cilantro, and a drizzle of salsa.

Pro tip: Squeeze fresh lime juice over the top before serving.

## Fun Facts

Carne Asada Tacos are a beloved street food in Mexico. The marinated and grilled steak is the star of the show, with vibrant flavors that shine through.

4
servings

300
calories
per
serving

3 hours
(include
s slow
cooking)

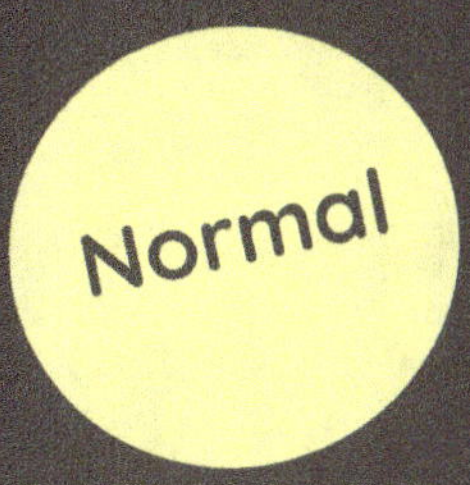


# Barbacoa Tacos

Barbacoa Tacos feature tender, slow-cooked beef with a kick of spices. This dish is rich in flavor and perfect for taco night.

## Ingredients:

- 2 pounds beef chuck roast
- 1 onion, diced
- 4 cloves garlic, minced
- 2 chipotle peppers in adobo sauce, minced
- 1 tablespoon ground cumin
- 1 tablespoon dried oregano
- 1 teaspoon paprika
- 1 teaspoon salt
- 1/2 teaspoon black pepper
- 1/2 cup beef broth
- 8 small corn tortillas
- Chopped fresh cilantro
- Salsa for drizzling

## Directions

1. In a slow cooker, combine beef chuck roast, diced onions, minced garlic, chipotle peppers, cumin, oregano, paprika, salt, pepper, and beef broth.
2. Cook on low for 6-8 hours until beef is tender and shreds easily.
3. Remove beef from the slow cooker and shred.
4. Warm corn tortillas in a dry skillet or microwave.
5. Assemble tacos with shredded beef, chopped cilantro, and a drizzle of salsa.

Pro tip: Add a squeeze of fresh lime juice for a burst of acidity.

## Fun Facts

Barbacoa Tacos are a flavorful option for meat lovers. The slow-cooked beef is infused with spices and perfect for a satisfying taco feast.

4 servings

280 calories per serving

40 minutes

# Tinga Tacos

Tinga Tacos are a smoky and spicy delight. Shredded chicken in a chipotle tomato sauce pairs perfectly with fresh toppings and avocado slices.

## Ingredients:

- 2 cups shredded chicken (cooked)
- 1 onion, thinly sliced
- 2 cloves garlic, minced
- 1 can (14 ounces) diced tomatoes
- 2 chipotle peppers in adobo sauce, minced
- 1 teaspoon dried oregano
- 1/2 teaspoon smoked paprika
- 8 small corn tortillas
- 1 avocado, sliced
- Chopped fresh cilantro
- Sour cream for drizzling
- Salt and pepper to taste

## Directions

1. In a skillet, sauté thinly sliced onions and minced garlic until onions are translucent.
2. Add shredded chicken, diced tomatoes, chipotle peppers, oregano, smoked paprika, salt, and pepper.
3. Simmer for 15-20 minutes until the sauce thickens.
4. Warm corn tortillas in a dry skillet or microwave.
5. Assemble tacos with tinga chicken, avocado slices, chopped cilantro, and a drizzle of sour cream.

Pro tip: Adjust the heat by adding more or fewer chipotle peppers.

## Fun Facts

Tinga Tacos are a smoky and spicy delight, featuring shredded chicken in a flavorful chipotle tomato sauce. They're a fiesta for your taste buds.

# Chapter 4:
# Bold Burritos & Enchiladas

2
servings

350
calories
per
serving

15
minutes

# Bean and Cheese Burrito

Bean and Cheese Burrito is a simple yet satisfying classic. It's a quick and hearty option filled with creamy refried beans and melted cheese.

## Ingredients:

- 1 cup refried beans
- 1 cup shredded cheddar cheese
- 2 large flour tortillas
- Salsa for serving (optional)

## Directions

1. Warm flour tortillas in a dry skillet or microwave.
2. Spread refried beans evenly over each tortilla.
3. Sprinkle shredded cheddar cheese on top of the beans.
4. Roll up the tortillas, tucking in the sides as you go.
5. Heat in a skillet or microwave until cheese is melted.
6. Serve with salsa if desired.

Pro tip: Customize with toppings like diced onions, jalapeños, or avocado slices.

## Fun Facts

Bean and Cheese Burrito is a quick and easy option, perfect for a satisfying meal on the go. It's a comfort food favorite.

2
servings

450
calories
per
serving

25
minutes

# Beef and Bean Burrito

Beef and Bean Burrito combines seasoned ground beef with creamy refried beans and melted cheese, wrapped in a warm tortilla.

## Ingredients:

- 1/2 pound ground beef
- 1/2 cup refried beans
- 1 cup shredded cheddar cheese
- 2 large flour tortillas
- Salsa for serving (optional)

## Directions

1. In a skillet, cook ground beef over medium-high heat until browned, breaking it into crumbles.
2. Warm flour tortillas in a dry skillet or microwave.
3. Spread refried beans evenly over each tortilla.
4. Spoon the cooked beef onto the beans.
5. Sprinkle shredded cheddar cheese on top of the beef.
6. Roll up the tortillas, tucking in the sides as you go.
7. Heat in a skillet or microwave until cheese is melted.
8. Serve with salsa if desired.

Pro tip: Add diced tomatoes and lettuce for extra freshness.

## Fun Facts

Beef and Bean Burrito is a hearty and flavorful option that combines the richness of beef with the creaminess of refried beans.

**4**
servings

**350**
calories
per
serving

**45**
minutes

# Chicken Enchiladas

Chicken Enchiladas are a delicious Tex-Mex favorite. Tender chicken, rolled in tortillas, smothered in red sauce, and baked to perfection.

## Ingredients:

- 2 cups shredded cooked chicken
- 1 cup diced onions
- 1 cup shredded Monterey Jack cheese
- 8 small corn tortillas
- 2 cups red enchilada sauce
- Chopped fresh cilantro for garnish (optional)
- Sour cream for serving (optional)

## Directions

1. Preheat the oven to 350°F (175°C).
2. In a skillet, sauté diced onions until translucent.
3. In a bowl, combine shredded chicken and sautéed onions.
4. Warm corn tortillas in a dry skillet or microwave.
5. Spoon chicken mixture onto each tortilla, sprinkle with shredded cheese, and roll up.
6. Place rolled enchiladas seam side down in a baking dish.
7. Pour red enchilada sauce over the top.
8. Bake for 25-30 minutes until bubbly and cheese is melted.
9. Garnish with chopped cilantro and serve with sour cream if desired.

Pro tip: Make extra sauce for extra sauciness.

## Fun Facts

Chicken Enchiladas are a comforting and flavorful dish, perfect for a family dinner or a gathering with friends.

4
servings

280
calories
per
serving

35
minutes

# Cheese Enchiladas

Cheese Enchiladas are a simple yet satisfying choice. Corn tortillas are filled with melty cheese, rolled, and topped with red sauce and more cheese.

## Ingredients:

- 2 cups shredded cheddar cheese
- 8 small corn tortillas
- 2 cups red enchilada sauce
- Chopped fresh cilantro for garnish (optional)
- Sour cream for serving (optional)

## Fun Facts

Cheese Enchiladas are a classic favorite, loved for their simplicity and the irresistible combination of cheese and red sauce.

## Directions

1. Preheat the oven to 350°F (175°C).
2. Warm corn tortillas in a dry skillet or microwave.
3. Spoon shredded cheddar cheese onto each tortilla and roll up.
4. Place rolled enchiladas seam side down in a baking dish.
5. Pour red enchilada sauce over the top.
6. Sprinkle with more shredded cheese.
7. Bake for 20-25 minutes until bubbly and cheese is melted.
8. Garnish with chopped cilantro and serve with sour cream if desired.

Pro tip: Add diced onions or black olives for extra flavor.

2
servings

300
calories
per
serving

25
minutes

# Veggie Burrito

Veggie Burrito is a flavorful meatless option. It's filled with sautéed vegetables, rice, beans, and cheese, all wrapped in a tortilla for a satisfying meal.

## Ingredients:

- 1 cup cooked rice
- 1 cup black beans, cooked
- 1 cup diced bell peppers (assorted colors)
- 1 cup sliced mushrooms
- 1/2 cup diced onions
- 1 cup shredded cheddar cheese
- 2 large flour tortillas
- Salsa for serving (optional)

## Directions

1. In a skillet, sauté diced onions, bell peppers, and sliced mushrooms until tender.
2. Warm flour tortillas in a dry skillet or microwave.
3. Spoon cooked rice, black beans, and sautéed vegetables onto each tortilla.
4. Sprinkle shredded cheddar cheese on top.
5. Roll up the tortillas, tucking in the sides as you go.
6. Heat in a skillet or microwave until cheese is melted.
7. Serve with salsa if desired.

Pro tip: Add avocado slices or guacamole for extra creaminess.

## Fun Facts

Veggie Burrito is a delicious and nutritious option, perfect for vegetarians and anyone looking for a meatless meal.

2
servings

400
calories
per
serving

20
minutes

# Breakfast Burrito

Breakfast Burrito is a hearty morning meal. Scrambled eggs, crispy bacon or sausage, and cheese are rolled up in a tortilla, creating a satisfying breakfast.

## Ingredients:

- 4 large eggs, scrambled
- 4 slices bacon or sausage links, cooked and crumbled
- 1 cup shredded cheddar cheese
- 2 large flour tortillas
- Salsa for serving (optional)

## Directions

1. In a skillet, scramble the eggs until cooked to your liking.
2. Warm flour tortillas in a dry skillet or microwave.
3. Divide scrambled eggs between the tortillas.
4. Sprinkle crumbled bacon or sausage on top.
5. Add shredded cheddar cheese.
6. Roll up the tortillas, tucking in the sides as you go.
7. Heat in a skillet or microwave until cheese is melted.
8. Serve with salsa if desired.

Pro tip: Add diced tomatoes or diced green chiles for extra flavor.

## Fun Facts

Breakfast Burrito is a hearty way to start your day, packed with protein and flavor. It's a satisfying breakfast option.

4
servings

380
calories
per
serving

45
minutes

# Beef Enchiladas

Beef Enchiladas are a savory delight. Seasoned ground beef, rolled in corn tortillas, and topped with red sauce and cheese, then baked to perfection.

## Ingredients:

- 1/2 pound ground beef
- 1 cup diced onions
- 1 cup shredded cheddar cheese
- 8 small corn tortillas
- 2 cups red enchilada sauce
- Chopped fresh cilantro for garnish (optional)
- Sour cream for serving (optional)

## Fun Facts

Beef Enchiladas are a savory and hearty dish, perfect for those who love the rich flavor of seasoned ground beef.

## Directions

1. Preheat the oven to 350°F (175°C).
2. In a skillet, cook ground beef over medium-high heat until browned, breaking it into crumbles.
3. Remove excess fat from the skillet.
4. Warm corn tortillas in a dry skillet or microwave.
5. Spoon cooked ground beef onto each tortilla, sprinkle with shredded cheddar cheese, and roll up.
6. Place rolled enchiladas seam side down in a baking dish.
7. Pour red enchilada sauce over the top.
8. Bake for 25-30 minutes until bubbly and cheese is melted.
9. Garnish with chopped cilantro and serve with sour cream if desired.

Pro tip: Add diced green chiles or jalapeños for a spicy kick.

2
servings

350
calories
per
serving

30
minutes

# Green Chile Chicken Burrito

Green Chile Chicken Burrito is a flavorful choice. It features tender chicken, green chiles, and cheese, all rolled up in a tortilla and baked to perfection.

## Ingredients:

- 1 cup cooked shredded chicken
- 1/2 cup diced green chiles
- 1 cup shredded Monterey Jack cheese
- 2 large flour tortillas
- 1/2 cup green enchilada sauce
- Salsa for serving (optional)

## Fun Facts

Green Chile Chicken Burrito is a delicious option for those who enjoy the mild heat of green chiles. It's a flavorful delight.

## Directions

1. Preheat the oven to 350°F (175°C).
2. Warm flour tortillas in a dry skillet or microwave.
3. In a bowl, combine shredded chicken and diced green chiles.
4. Spoon the chicken and chile mixture onto each tortilla.
5. Sprinkle shredded Monterey Jack cheese on top.
6. Roll up the tortillas, tucking in the sides as you go.
7. Place rolled burritos seam side down in a baking dish.
8. Pour green enchilada sauce over the top.
9. Bake for 20-25 minutes until bubbly and cheese is melted.
10. Serve with salsa if desired.

Pro tip: Add diced tomatoes or chopped cilantro for extra freshness.

4 servings

320 calories per serving

40 minutes

# Shrimp Enchiladas

Shrimp Enchiladas are a seafood lover's dream. Succulent shrimp, rolled in corn tortillas, and topped with a creamy sauce, then baked to perfection.

## Ingredients:

- 1 pound large shrimp, peeled and deveined
- 1/2 cup diced onions
- 1/2 cup diced bell peppers (assorted colors)
- 1 cup shredded Monterey Jack cheese
- 8 small corn tortillas
- 2 cups creamy seafood or Alfredo sauce
- Chopped fresh cilantro for garnish (optional)
- Lemon wedges for serving (optional)

## Fun Facts

Shrimp Enchiladas offer a taste of the sea with creamy and indulgent flavors. They're perfect for a special occasion dinner.

## Directions

1. Preheat the oven to 350°F (175°C).
2. In a skillet, sauté diced onions and bell peppers until tender.
3. Add peeled and deveined shrimp and cook until pink and opaque, about 2-3 minutes per side.
4. Warm corn tortillas in a dry skillet or microwave.
5. Spoon cooked shrimp onto each tortilla, sprinkle with shredded Monterey Jack cheese, and roll up.
6. Place rolled enchiladas seam side down in a baking dish.
7. Pour creamy seafood or Alfredo sauce over the top.
8. Bake for 20-25 minutes until bubbly and cheese is melted.
9. Garnish with chopped cilantro and serve with lemon wedges if desired.

Pro tip: Add a pinch of cayenne pepper for a touch of heat.

4
servings

290
calories
per
serving

45
minutes

# Sweet Potato and Black Bean Enchiladas

Sweet Potato and Black Bean Enchiladas are a vegetarian delight. Roasted sweet potato, black beans, and cheese are rolled in corn tortillas and topped with red sauce.

## Ingredients:

- 2 cups roasted sweet potato cubes
- 1 cup cooked black beans
- 1 cup diced red onion
- 1 cup shredded cheddar cheese
- 8 small corn tortillas
- 2 cups red enchilada sauce
- Chopped fresh cilantro for garnish (optional)
- Sour cream for serving (optional)

## Directions

1. Preheat the oven to 350°F (175°C).
2. Warm corn tortillas in a dry skillet or microwave.
3. In a bowl, combine roasted sweet potato cubes, cooked black beans, and diced red onion.
4. Spoon the sweet potato and black bean mixture onto each tortilla.
5. Sprinkle shredded cheddar cheese on top.
6. Roll up the tortillas, tucking in the sides as you go.
7. Place rolled enchiladas seam side down in a baking dish.
8. Pour red enchilada sauce over the top.
9. Bake for 20-25 minutes until bubbly and cheese is melted.
10. Garnish with chopped cilantro and serve with sour cream if desired.

Pro tip: Add diced green chiles for a mild heat.

## Fun Facts

Sweet Potato and Black Bean Enchiladas are a vegetarian delight, packed with flavor and hearty ingredients. They're perfect for those seeking a meatless meal option.

# We have a small favor to ask

My Culinary Comrades,

As we embark on this exhilarating journey through the heart of Mexico, exploring its rich tapestry of flavors with our "Mexican Fiesta with 5 Ingredients" cookbook, I can't help but feel a profound sense of gratitude for the pleasure of your company. Mexican cuisine is a vibrant fiesta of tastes and traditions, and I'm truly delighted to be your guide on this gastronomic adventure.

But, before we dive back into our tantalizing recipes, I must pause for a moment to talk about something crucial. In the realm of cookbooks and culinary explorations, reviews are akin to the spices and seasonings that add depth and character to a dish. They're the magic that makes our culinary creations come to life, and they're often hard to come by, especially for small, passionate publishers like us.

So here's my humble request: if you've enjoyed your experience so far and found our recipes as delightful as I intended them to be, please consider taking a moment to leave a review. It's a simple process; just go back to your app or the platform where you purchased this book, click on the review button, assign us a star rating, and perhaps share a brief sentence or two about your culinary escapades with this cookbook. Your reviews are not just valuable; they're the lifeblood of our culinary journey.

Your insights, your appreciation, your constructive feedback - they all serve as signposts on our path to becoming better culinary adventurers. I read every single review personally, as does our dedicated team, and your words never fail to inspire and guide us.

And now, as we return to the heart of Mexico through these recipes, let our culinary adventure continue. May the coming pages be filled with the sizzle of a hot skillet, the aroma of freshly ground spices, and the joy of bringing authentic Mexican dishes to life in your own kitchen.

With sincere gratitude and a shared love for the flavors of Mexico,
**Garden of Grapes**

# Chapter 5:
# Hearty Quesadillas & Nachos

1
quesadill
a

250
calories

10
minutes

# Cheese Quesadilla

**Easy**

Cheese Quesadilla is a simple yet comforting classic. It's a quick and gooey delight with melted cheese, all wrapped in a warm tortilla.

## Ingredients:

- 1 large flour tortilla
- 1 cup shredded cheddar cheese
- Salsa for serving (optional)

## Directions

1. Place a large flour tortilla in a dry skillet over medium heat.
2. Sprinkle shredded cheddar cheese evenly over half of the tortilla.
3. Fold the other half of the tortilla over the cheese to create a half-moon shape.
4. Cook for 2-3 minutes per side until the tortilla is golden and the cheese is melted.
5. Slice into wedges and serve with salsa if desired.

Pro tip: Customize with additional fillings like diced green chiles or jalapeños.

## Fun Facts

Cheese Quesadilla is a quick and satisfying snack or meal option, perfect for cheese lovers of all ages.

1
quesadill
a

320
calories

20
minutes

# Chicken Quesadilla

Chicken Quesadilla features tender chicken, melted cheese, and optional veggies, all folded in a tortilla.

## Ingredients:

- 1 large flour tortilla
- 1/2 cup cooked shredded chicken
- 1/2 cup shredded cheddar cheese
- 1/4 cup diced bell peppers (assorted colors, optional)
- Salsa for serving (optional)

## Directions

1. Place a large flour tortilla in a dry skillet over medium heat.
2. Sprinkle shredded cheddar cheese evenly over half of the tortilla.
3. Add cooked shredded chicken (and diced bell peppers if using).
4. Fold the other half of the tortilla over the filling to create a half-moon shape.
5. Cook for 2-3 minutes per side until the tortilla is golden and the cheese is melted.
6. Slice into wedges and serve with salsa if desired.

Pro tip: Add a dash of hot sauce for extra flavor.

## Fun Facts

Chicken Quesadilla is a satisfying choice that combines the goodness of chicken and melted cheese in a crispy tortilla.

1
quesadill
a

350
calories

20
minutes

# Beef Quesadilla

Beef Quesadilla features seasoned ground beef, melted cheese, and optional veggies, all folded in a tortilla.

## Ingredients:

- 1 large flour tortilla
- 1/2 cup seasoned cooked ground beef
- 1/2 cup shredded cheddar cheese
- 1/4 cup diced onions (optional)
- Salsa for serving (optional)

## Directions

1. Place a large flour tortilla in a dry skillet over medium heat.
2. Sprinkle shredded cheddar cheese evenly over half of the tortilla.
3. Add seasoned cooked ground beef (and diced onions if using).
4. Fold the other half of the tortilla over the filling to create a half-moon shape.
5. Cook for 2-3 minutes per side until the tortilla is golden and the cheese is melted.
6. Slice into wedges and serve with salsa if desired.

Pro tip: Customize with your favorite taco toppings.

## Fun Facts

Beef Quesadilla is a flavorful and hearty choice, perfect for those who love the savory taste of seasoned ground beef.

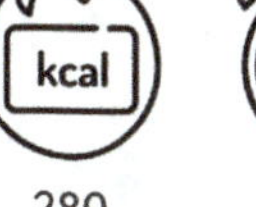

1 quesadilla

280 calories

15 minutes

# Veggie Quesadilla

Veggie Quesadilla is a meatless delight. It's filled with sautéed vegetables, melted cheese, and wrapped in a warm tortilla.

## Ingredients:

- 1 large flour tortilla
- 1 cup sliced bell peppers (assorted colors)
- 1/2 cup sliced mushrooms
- 1/4 cup diced onions
- 1 cup shredded cheddar cheese
- Salsa for serving (optional)

## Directions

1. Place a large flour tortilla in a dry skillet over medium heat.
2. Sprinkle shredded cheddar cheese evenly over half of the tortilla.
3. In a skillet, sauté sliced bell peppers, mushrooms, and diced onions until tender.
4. Spoon the sautéed vegetables over the cheese.
5. Fold the other half of the tortilla over the filling to create a half-moon shape.
6. Cook for 2-3 minutes per side until the tortilla is golden and the cheese is melted.
7. Slice into wedges and serve with salsa if desired.

Pro tip: Add diced tomatoes or avocado slices for extra freshness.

## Fun Facts

Veggie Quesadilla is a delicious and nutritious option, perfect for vegetarians and anyone looking for a meatless meal.

1
quesadilla

330
calories

20
minutes

# Shrimp Quesadilla

Shrimp Quesadilla is a seafood lover's treat. It features succulent shrimp, melted cheese, and optional veggies, all folded in a tortilla.

## Ingredients:

- 1 large flour tortilla
- 1/2 cup cooked large shrimp, peeled and deveined
- 1/2 cup shredded Monterey Jack cheese
- 1/4 cup diced bell peppers (assorted colors, optional)
- Salsa for serving (optional)

## Directions

1. Place a large flour tortilla in a dry skillet over medium heat.
2. Sprinkle shredded Monterey Jack cheese evenly over half of the tortilla.
3. Add cooked large shrimp (and diced bell peppers if using).
4. Fold the other half of the tortilla over the filling to create a half-moon shape.
5. Cook for 2-3 minutes per side until the tortilla is golden and the cheese is melted.
6. Slice into wedges and serve with salsa if desired.

Pro tip: Add a squeeze of fresh lime juice for extra zing.

## Fun Facts

Shrimp Quesadilla offers a taste of the sea with succulent shrimp and melted cheese. It's a delightful seafood option.

4
servings

400
calories
per
serving

20
minutes

# Loaded Nachos

Loaded Nachos are a crowd-pleasing favorite. Crispy tortilla chips are piled high with seasoned ground beef, cheese, and a variety of toppings.

## Ingredients:

- 1 bag (about 10-12 ounces) tortilla chips
- 1/2 pound seasoned cooked ground beef
- 2 cups shredded cheddar cheese
- 1/2 cup diced tomatoes
- 1/4 cup sliced black olives
- 1/4 cup diced onions
- 1/4 cup sliced jalapeños
- Sour cream and salsa for serving

## Directions

1. Preheat the oven to 350°F (175°C).
2. Spread a layer of tortilla chips on a baking sheet or oven-safe platter.
3. Sprinkle seasoned cooked ground beef evenly over the chips.
4. Scatter shredded cheddar cheese on top.
5. Add diced tomatoes, sliced black olives, diced onions, and sliced jalapeños.
6. Bake for 10-12 minutes until cheese is melted and nachos are heated through.
7. Serve with sour cream and salsa.

Pro tip: Customize with your favorite toppings like guacamole or diced green chiles.

## Fun Facts

Loaded Nachos are the ultimate snack or party food, perfect for sharing and piling on your favorite toppings.

4
servings

320
calories
per
serving

20
minutes

# Veggie Nachos

Veggie Nachos are a healthier twist on the classic. Tortilla chips are loaded with sautéed veggies, black beans, and cheese, then baked to perfection.

## Ingredients:

- 1 bag (about 10-12 ounces) tortilla chips
- 1 cup sliced bell peppers (assorted colors)
- 1/2 cup sliced mushrooms
- 1/4 cup diced onions
- 1 cup cooked black beans
- 2 cups shredded cheddar cheese
- Salsa for serving (optional)

## Directions

1. Preheat the oven to 350°F (175°C).
2. Spread a layer of tortilla chips on a baking sheet or oven-safe platter.
3. In a skillet, sauté sliced bell peppers, mushrooms, and diced onions until tender.
4. Scatter sautéed veggies and cooked black beans evenly over the chips.
5. Sprinkle shredded cheddar cheese on top.
6. Bake for 10-12 minutes until cheese is melted and nachos are heated through.
7. Serve with salsa.

Pro tip: Add a dollop of Greek yogurt or sour cream for extra creaminess.

## Fun Facts

Veggie Nachos offer a nutritious twist on a classic snack, packed with sautéed veggies and black beans.

**4 servings**

**380 calories per serving**

**25 minutes**

# Beef Nachos

Beef Nachos feature seasoned ground beef, cheese, and classic toppings piled on crispy tortilla chips.

## Ingredients:

- 1 bag (about 10-12 ounces) tortilla chips
- 1/2 pound seasoned cooked ground beef
- 2 cups shredded cheddar cheese
- 1/2 cup diced tomatoes
- 1/4 cup sliced black olives
- 1/4 cup diced onions
- 1/4 cup sliced jalapeños
- Sour cream and salsa for serving

## Directions

1. Preheat the oven to 350°F (175°C).
2. Spread a layer of tortilla chips on a baking sheet or oven-safe platter.
3. Sprinkle seasoned cooked ground beef evenly over the chips.
4. Scatter shredded cheddar cheese on top.
5. Add diced tomatoes, sliced black olives, diced onions, and sliced jalapeños.
6. Bake for 10-12 minutes until cheese is melted and nachos are heated through.
7. Serve with sour cream and salsa.

Pro tip: Add guacamole or diced green chiles for extra flavor.

## Fun Facts

Beef Nachos are a hearty and satisfying snack, perfect for game day or a casual get-together.

4
servings

350
calories
per
serving

25
minutes

# Chicken Nachos

Chicken Nachos feature tender chicken, cheese, and classic toppings piled on crispy tortilla chips.

## Ingredients:

- 1 bag (about 10-12 ounces) tortilla chips
- 1/2 cup cooked shredded chicken
- 2 cups shredded cheddar cheese
- 1/2 cup diced tomatoes
- 1/4 cup sliced black olives
- 1/4 cup diced onions
- 1/4 cup sliced jalapeños
- Sour cream and salsa for serving

## Directions

1. Preheat the oven to 350°F (175°C).
2. Spread a layer of tortilla chips on a baking sheet or oven-safe platter.
3. Sprinkle cooked shredded chicken evenly over the chips.
4. Scatter shredded cheddar cheese on top.
5. Add diced tomatoes, sliced black olives, diced onions, and sliced jalapeños.
6. Bake for 10-12 minutes until cheese is melted and nachos are heated through.
7. Serve with sour cream and salsa.

Pro tip: Drizzle with hot sauce for extra kick.

## Fun Facts

Chicken Nachos are a tasty twist on the classic, featuring tender chicken and all the favorite nacho toppings.

**4 servings**

**300 calories per serving**

**20 minutes**

# Black Bean Nachos

Black Bean Nachos are a vegetarian delight. Tortilla chips are loaded with black beans, cheese, and classic toppings, then baked to perfection.

## Ingredients:

- 1 bag (about 10-12 ounces) tortilla chips
- 1 cup cooked black beans
- 2 cups shredded cheddar cheese
- 1/2 cup diced tomatoes
- 1/4 cup sliced black olives
- 1/4 cup diced onions
- 1/4 cup sliced jalapeños
- Sour cream and salsa for serving (optional)

## Directions

1. Preheat the oven to 350°F (175°C).
2. Spread a layer of tortilla chips on a baking sheet or oven-safe platter.
3. Scatter cooked black beans evenly over the chips.
4. Sprinkle shredded cheddar cheese on top.
5. Add diced tomatoes, sliced black olives, diced onions, and sliced jalapeños.
6. Bake for 10-12 minutes until cheese is melted and nachos are heated through.
7. Serve with sour cream and salsa.

Pro tip: Add diced avocado for extra creaminess.

## Fun Facts

Black Bean Nachos are a delicious and nutritious option, perfect for vegetarians and anyone looking for a meatless snack.

# Chapter 6:
## Flavorful Fajitas & Skillets

4
servings

320
calories
per
serving

30
minutes

# Chicken Fajitas

Chicken Fajitas are a sizzling sensation. Tender chicken, bell peppers, and onions are cooked in flavorful spices and served with warm tortillas.

## Ingredients:

- 1 pound boneless, skinless chicken breasts, sliced into strips
- 2 bell peppers (assorted colors), sliced
- 1 large onion, sliced
- 2 cloves garlic, minced
- 2 tablespoons olive oil
- 1 teaspoon chili powder
- 1/2 teaspoon ground cumin
- 1/2 teaspoon smoked paprika
- 1/4 teaspoon cayenne pepper (adjust to taste)
- Salt and pepper to taste
- 8 small flour tortillas
- Sour cream and salsa for serving (optional)

## Directions

1. In a large skillet, heat olive oil over medium-high heat.
2. Add sliced chicken and cook until browned and cooked through.
3. Remove chicken from the skillet and set aside.
4. In the same skillet, add sliced bell peppers and onions.
5. Sauté until they start to soften.
6. Add minced garlic and cook for another minute.
7. Return the cooked chicken to the skillet.
8. Sprinkle with chili powder, ground cumin, smoked paprika, cayenne pepper, salt, and pepper.
9. Cook for a few more minutes until everything is heated through and well-coated with spices.
10. Serve the chicken and veggie mixture with warm flour tortillas.
11. Offer sour cream and salsa for garnish if desired.

Pro tip: Squeeze fresh lime juice over the fajitas for a burst of citrus flavor.

## Fun Facts

Chicken Fajitas are a sizzling and flavorful Tex-Mex classic, perfect for a fun and interactive meal.

4
servings

380
calories
per
serving

40
minutes

# Steak Fajitas

Steak Fajitas are a meat lover's delight. Sliced steak, bell peppers, and onions are cooked to perfection and served with warm tortillas.

## Ingredients:

- 1 pound flank steak, thinly sliced against the grain
- 2 bell peppers (assorted colors), sliced
- 1 large onion, sliced
- 2 cloves garlic, minced
- 2 tablespoons olive oil
- 1 teaspoon chili powder
- 1/2 teaspoon ground cumin
- 1/2 teaspoon smoked paprika
- 1/4 teaspoon cayenne pepper (adjust to taste)
- Salt and pepper to taste
- 8 small flour tortillas
- Sour cream and salsa for serving (optional)

## Directions

1. In a large skillet, heat olive oil over medium-high heat.
2. Add sliced flank steak and cook until browned to your liking.
3. Remove steak from the skillet and set aside.
4. In the same skillet, add sliced bell peppers and onions.
5. Sauté until they start to soften.
6. Add minced garlic and cook for another minute.
7. Return the cooked steak to the skillet.
8. Sprinkle with chili powder, ground cumin, smoked paprika, cayenne pepper, salt, and pepper.
9. Cook for a few more minutes until everything is heated through and well-coated with spices.
10. Serve the steak and veggie mixture with warm flour tortillas.
11. Offer sour cream and salsa for garnish if desired.

Pro tip: Marinate the steak in lime juice and olive oil for extra flavor.

## Fun Facts

Steak Fajitas are a hearty and satisfying dish, perfect for those who crave the bold flavor of grilled steak.

4
servings

300
calories
per
serving

25
minutes

# Shrimp Fajitas

Shrimp Fajitas offer a taste of the sea. Succulent shrimp, bell peppers, and onions are cooked in zesty spices and served with warm tortillas.

## Ingredients:

- 1 pound large shrimp, peeled and deveined
- 2 bell peppers (assorted colors), sliced
- 1 large onion, sliced
- 2 cloves garlic, minced
- 2 tablespoons olive oil
- 1 teaspoon chili powder
- 1/2 teaspoon ground cumin
- 1/2 teaspoon smoked paprika
- 1/4 teaspoon cayenne pepper (adjust to taste)
- Salt and pepper to taste
- 8 small flour tortillas
- Sour cream and salsa for serving (optional)

## Directions

1. In a large skillet, heat olive oil over medium-high heat.
2. Add peeled and deveined shrimp and cook until pink and opaque, about 2-3 minutes per side.
3. Remove shrimp from the skillet and set aside.
4. In the same skillet, add sliced bell peppers and onions.
5. Sauté until they start to soften.
6. Add minced garlic and cook for another minute.
7. Return the cooked shrimp to the skillet.
8. Sprinkle with chili powder, ground cumin, smoked paprika, cayenne pepper, salt, and pepper.
9. Cook for a few more minutes until everything is heated through and well-coated with spices.
10. Serve the shrimp and veggie mixture with warm flour tortillas.
11. Offer sour cream and salsa for garnish if desired.

Pro tip: Add a sprinkle of fresh cilantro for extra freshness.

## Fun Facts

Shrimp Fajitas are a delightful seafood option, offering succulent shrimp with a burst of zesty flavors.

4
servings

250
calories
per
serving

25
minutes

# Veggie Fajitas

Veggie Fajitas are a vegetarian delight. Sautéed bell peppers, onions, and mushrooms are seasoned to perfection and served with warm tortillas.

## Ingredients:

- 2 bell peppers (assorted colors), sliced
- 1 large onion, sliced
- 1 cup sliced mushrooms
- 2 cloves garlic, minced
- 2 tablespoons olive oil
- 1 teaspoon chili powder
- 1/2 teaspoon ground cumin
- 1/2 teaspoon smoked paprika
- 1/4 teaspoon cayenne pepper (adjust to taste)
- Salt and pepper to taste
- 8 small flour tortillas
- Sour cream and salsa for serving (optional)

## Directions

1. In a large skillet, heat olive oil over medium-high heat.
2. Add sliced bell peppers, onions, and mushrooms.
3. Sauté until they start to soften.
4. Add minced garlic and cook for another minute.
5. Sprinkle with chili powder, ground cumin, smoked paprika, cayenne pepper, salt, and pepper.
6. Cook for a few more minutes until the veggies are tender and well-coated with spices.
7. Serve the sautéed veggie mixture with warm flour tortillas.
8. Offer sour cream and salsa for garnish if desired.

Pro tip: Add sliced avocado for extra creaminess.

## Fun Facts

Veggie Fajitas are a flavorful and nutritious option, perfect for vegetarians and anyone looking for a meatless meal.

4
servings

350
calories
per
serving

30
minutes

# Beef Skillet

Beef Skillet is a savory one-pan wonder. Seasoned ground beef, bell peppers, onions, and rice come together in a hearty and satisfying dish.

## Ingredients:

- 1 pound ground beef
- 1 large onion, chopped
- 2 cloves garlic, minced
- 1 bell pepper (any color), chopped
- 1 cup long-grain white rice
- 1 can (14 ounces) diced tomatoes, undrained
- 1 cup beef broth
- 1 teaspoon chili powder
- 1/2 teaspoon ground cumin
- Salt and pepper to taste
- Chopped fresh cilantro for garnish (optional)

## Directions

1. In a large skillet, cook ground beef over medium-high heat until browned, breaking it into crumbles.
2. Remove excess fat from the skillet.
3. Add chopped onion, minced garlic, and chopped bell pepper to the skillet.
4. Sauté until the vegetables start to soften.
5. Stir in long-grain white rice, diced tomatoes (with their juice), beef broth, chili powder, ground cumin, salt, and pepper.
6. Bring the mixture to a boil, then reduce heat to low.
7. Cover and simmer for 20-25 minutes, or until the rice is tender and the liquid is absorbed.
8. Garnish with chopped fresh cilantro if desired.

Pro tip: Customize with your favorite toppings like shredded cheese or avocado slices.

## Fun Facts

Beef Skillet is a hearty and satisfying one-pan meal that's perfect for busy weeknight dinners.

4
servings

320
calories
per
serving

30
minutes

# Chicken Skillet

Chicken Skillet is a flavorful one-pan dish. Tender chicken breasts, bell peppers, onions, and rice are cooked to perfection in a savory sauce.

## Ingredients:

- 4 boneless, skinless chicken breasts
- 1 large onion, chopped
- 2 cloves garlic, minced
- 1 bell pepper (any color), chopped
- 1 cup long-grain white rice
- 1 can (14 ounces) diced tomatoes, undrained
- 1 cup chicken broth
- 1 teaspoon chili powder
- 1/2 teaspoon ground cumin
- Salt and pepper to taste
- Chopped fresh cilantro for garnish (optional)

## Directions

1. In a large skillet, heat a bit of oil over medium-high heat.
2. Add chicken breasts and cook until browned on both sides and no longer pink in the center.
3. Remove chicken from the skillet and set aside.
4. In the same skillet, add chopped onion, minced garlic, and chopped bell pepper.
5. Sauté until the vegetables start to soften.
6. Stir in long-grain white rice, diced tomatoes (with their juice), chicken broth, chili powder, ground cumin, salt, and pepper.
7. Bring the mixture to a boil, then reduce heat to low.
8. Return the cooked chicken to the skillet, placing it on top of the rice mixture.
9. Cover and simmer for 20-25 minutes, or until the rice is tender and the chicken is cooked through.
10. Garnish with chopped fresh cilantro if desired.

Pro tip: Add a squeeze of fresh lime juice for extra zest.

## Fun Facts

Chicken Skillet is a flavorful and satisfying one-pan meal that's perfect for a family dinner.

4
servings

300
calories
per
serving

25
minutes

# Shrimp Skillet

Shrimp Skillet is a seafood lover's dream. Succulent shrimp, bell peppers, onions, and rice are cooked in a savory sauce for a delightful meal.

## Ingredients:

- 1 pound large shrimp, peeled and deveined
- 1 large onion, chopped
- 2 cloves garlic, minced
- 1 bell pepper (any color), chopped
- 1 cup long-grain white rice
- 1 can (14 ounces) diced tomatoes, undrained
- 1 cup chicken broth
- 1 teaspoon chili powder
- 1/2 teaspoon ground cumin
- Salt and pepper to taste
- Chopped fresh parsley for garnish (optional)

## Directions

1. In a large skillet, heat a bit of oil over medium-high heat.
2. Add peeled and deveined shrimp and cook until pink and opaque, about 2-3 minutes per side.
3. Remove shrimp from the skillet and set aside.
4. In the same skillet, add chopped onion, minced garlic, and chopped bell pepper.
5. Sauté until the vegetables start to soften.
6. Stir in long-grain white rice, diced tomatoes (with their juice), chicken broth, chili powder, ground cumin, salt, and pepper.
7. Bring the mixture to a boil, then reduce heat to low.
8. Return the cooked shrimp to the skillet, placing them on top of the rice mixture.
9. Cover and simmer for 20-25 minutes, or until the rice is tender and the shrimp is heated through.
10. Garnish with chopped fresh parsley if desired.

Pro tip: Add a dash of hot sauce for extra heat.

## Fun Facts

Shrimp Skillet is a seafood lover's delight, featuring succulent shrimp and a savory rice and veggie medley.

**4**
servings

**250**
calories
per
serving

**25**
minutes

# Veggie Skillet

Veggie Skillet is a vegetarian delight. Sautéed bell peppers, onions, mushrooms, and rice come together in a flavorful one-pan dish.

## Ingredients:

- 2 bell peppers (assorted colors), sliced
- 1 large onion, sliced
- 1 cup sliced mushrooms
- 2 cloves garlic, minced
- 2 tablespoons olive oil
- 1 cup long-grain white rice
- 1 can (14 ounces) diced tomatoes, undrained
- 1 cup vegetable broth
- 1 teaspoon chili powder
- 1/2 teaspoon ground cumin
- Salt and pepper to taste
- Chopped fresh basil for garnish (optional)

## Directions

1. In a large skillet, heat olive oil over medium-high heat.
2. Add sliced bell peppers, onions, and mushrooms.
3. Sauté until they start to soften.
4. Add minced garlic and cook for another minute.
5. Stir in long-grain white rice, diced tomatoes (with their juice), vegetable broth, chili powder, ground cumin, salt, and pepper.
6. Bring the mixture to a boil, then reduce heat to low.
7. Cover and simmer for 20-25 minutes, or until the rice is tender.
8. Garnish with chopped fresh basil if desired.

Pro tip: Customize with your favorite vegetables like zucchini or corn.

## Fun Facts

Veggie Skillet is a flavorful and nutritious one-pan meal, perfect for vegetarians and anyone looking for a meatless option.

4
servings

330
calories
per
serving

30
minutes

# Beef and Bean Skillet

Beef and Bean Skillet is a hearty one-pan meal. Seasoned ground beef, black beans, and rice are cooked to perfection for a satisfying dish.

## Ingredients:

- 1 pound ground beef
- 1 large onion, chopped
- 2 cloves garlic, minced
- 1 cup long-grain white rice
- 1 can (14 ounces) black beans, drained and rinsed
- 1 can (14 ounces) diced tomatoes, undrained
- 1 cup beef broth
- 1 teaspoon chili powder
- 1/2 teaspoon ground cumin
- Salt and pepper to taste
- Chopped fresh cilantro for garnish (optional)

## Directions

1. In a large skillet, cook ground beef over medium-high heat until browned, breaking it into crumbles.
2. Remove excess fat from the skillet.
3. Add chopped onion and minced garlic to the skillet.
4. Sauté until the onion is translucent.
5. Stir in long-grain white rice, black beans, diced tomatoes (with their juice), beef broth, chili powder, ground cumin, salt, and pepper.
6. Bring the mixture to a boil, then reduce heat to low.
7. Cover and simmer for 20-25 minutes, or until the rice is tender and the liquid is absorbed.
8. Garnish with chopped fresh cilantro if desired.

Pro tip: Top with shredded cheese for extra richness.

## Fun Facts

Beef and Bean Skillet is a hearty and satisfying one-pan meal, perfect for meat and bean lovers.

4
servings

360
calories
per
serving

30
minutes

# Chorizo Skillet

Chorizo Skillet is a spicy and flavorful dish. Spicy chorizo sausage, bell peppers, onions, and rice are cooked to perfection for a bold meal.

## Ingredients:

- 1 pound chorizo sausage, casings removed
- 1 large onion, chopped
- 2 cloves garlic, minced
- 1 bell pepper (any color), chopped
- 1 cup long-grain white rice
- 1 can (14 ounces) diced tomatoes, undrained
- 1 cup chicken broth
- 1/2 teaspoon smoked paprika
- Salt and pepper to taste
- Chopped fresh cilantro for garnish (optional)

## Fun Facts

Chorizo Skillet is a bold and spicy one-pan meal, perfect for those who love the flavors of chorizo sausage.

## Directions

1. In a large skillet, cook chorizo sausage over medium-high heat, breaking it into crumbles, until browned and cooked through.
2. Remove excess fat from the skillet.
3. Add chopped onion, minced garlic, and chopped bell pepper to the skillet.
4. Sauté until the vegetables start to soften.
5. Stir in long-grain white rice, diced tomatoes (with their juice), chicken broth, smoked paprika, salt, and pepper.
6. Bring the mixture to a boil, then reduce heat to low.
7. Cover and simmer for 20-25 minutes, or until the rice is tender and the liquid is absorbed.
8. Garnish with chopped fresh cilantro if desired.

Pro tip: Add a splash of hot sauce for extra heat.

# Chapter 7:
## Scrumptious Sides & Salads

**4 servings**

**220 calories per serving**

**25 minutes**

# Mexican Rice

Mexican Rice is a flavorful side dish. Long-grain rice is cooked with tomatoes, onions, and spices for a delightful accompaniment to your meal.

## Ingredients:

- 1 cup long-grain white rice
- 1 can (14 ounces) diced tomatoes, undrained
- 1/2 cup chopped onion
- 2 cloves garlic, minced
- 1/2 teaspoon ground cumin
- 1/2 teaspoon chili powder
- 1/2 teaspoon smoked paprika
- 2 cups chicken broth
- Salt and pepper to taste
- Chopped fresh cilantro for garnish (optional)

## Fun Facts

Mexican Rice is a classic and versatile side dish that pairs well with a variety of Mexican and Tex-Mex dishes.

## Directions

1. In a large skillet, heat a bit of oil over medium-high heat.
2. Add chopped onion and minced garlic to the skillet.
3. Sauté until the onion is translucent.
4. Stir in long-grain white rice and cook for 2-3 minutes until lightly toasted.
5. Add diced tomatoes (with their juice), ground cumin, chili powder, smoked paprika, chicken broth, salt, and pepper.
6. Bring the mixture to a boil, then reduce heat to low.
7. Cover and simmer for 15-20 minutes, or until the rice is tender and the liquid is absorbed.
8. Fluff the rice with a fork and garnish with chopped fresh cilantro if desired.

Pro tip: Add a squeeze of fresh lime juice for extra zest.

**4 servings**

**180 calories per serving**

**15 minutes**

# Refried Beans

Refried Beans are a creamy side dish. Pinto beans are mashed and cooked with onions, garlic, and spices for a comforting addition to your meal.

## Ingredients:

- 2 cans (15 ounces each) pinto beans, drained and rinsed
- 1/2 cup chopped onion
- 2 cloves garlic, minced
- 2 tablespoons vegetable oil
- 1/2 teaspoon ground cumin
- Salt and pepper to taste
- Grated cheddar cheese and chopped fresh cilantro for garnish (optional)

## Fun Facts

Refried Beans are a comforting and creamy side dish that's a staple in Mexican cuisine.

## Directions

1. In a large skillet, heat vegetable oil over medium-high heat.
2. Add chopped onion and minced garlic to the skillet.
3. Sauté until the onion is translucent.
4. Add drained and rinsed pinto beans to the skillet.
5. Mash the beans with a potato masher or the back of a spoon.
6. Stir in ground cumin, salt, and pepper.
7. Cook for 5-7 minutes, stirring occasionally, until the beans are heated through and creamy.
8. Garnish with grated cheddar cheese and chopped fresh cilantro if desired.

Pro tip: Customize with a dollop of sour cream or sliced jalapeños for extra flavor.

4
servings

250
calories
per
serving

20
minutes

# Elote

Elote, or Mexican Street Corn, is a classic street food. Grilled corn on the cob is slathered with mayo, cheese, chili powder, and lime for a mouthwatering treat.

## Ingredients:

- 4 ears of corn, husked
- 1/4 cup mayonnaise
- 1/2 cup crumbled cotija cheese
- 1 teaspoon chili powder (adjust to taste)
- 4 lime wedges

## Directions

1. Preheat a grill or grill pan to medium-high heat.
2. Grill the husked ears of corn, turning occasionally, until they are charred and cooked through, about 10 minutes.
3. Remove the corn from the grill.
4. Spread each ear of corn with mayonnaise.
5. Roll the corn in crumbled cotija cheese, pressing gently to adhere.
6. Sprinkle with chili powder and serve with lime wedges for squeezing over the top.

Pro tip: Customize with a sprinkle of chopped cilantro for extra freshness.

## Fun Facts

Elote is a beloved Mexican street food that's both savory and satisfying, perfect for summer grilling.

4
servings

180
calories
per
serving

15
minutes

# Mexican Street Corn Salad

Mexican Street Corn Salad is a deconstructed elote. Grilled corn kernels are tossed with mayo, cheese, chili powder, and lime for a delightful salad.

## Ingredients:

- 4 cups grilled corn kernels (from about 4 ears of corn)
- 1/4 cup mayonnaise
- 1/2 cup crumbled cotija cheese
- 1 teaspoon chili powder (adjust to taste)
- Juice of 2 limes
- Chopped fresh cilantro for garnish (optional)

## Directions

1. In a large bowl, combine grilled corn kernels and mayonnaise.
2. Toss until the corn is evenly coated with the mayo.
3. Sprinkle crumbled cotija cheese over the corn and toss again.
4. Season with chili powder and squeeze lime juice over the top.
5. Toss to combine.
6. Garnish with chopped fresh cilantro if desired.

Pro tip: Add diced red onion or jalapeño for an extra kick.

## Fun Facts

Mexican Street Corn Salad is a refreshing and zesty twist on traditional elote, perfect for picnics and barbecues.

4
servings

220
calories
per
serving

20
minutes

# Cilantro Lime Rice

Cilantro Lime Rice is a fragrant side dish. Long-grain rice is cooked with fresh cilantro and lime juice for a burst of flavor.

## Ingredients:

- 1 cup long-grain white rice
- 2 cups water
- 1/2 cup fresh cilantro leaves, chopped
- Juice of 2 limes
- Salt to taste
- Lime wedges for garnish (optional)

## Directions

1. In a medium saucepan, combine long-grain white rice and water.
2. Bring to a boil, then reduce heat to low.
3. Cover and simmer for 15-18 minutes, or until the rice is tender and the liquid is absorbed.
4. Remove the saucepan from heat.
5. Fluff the rice with a fork.
6. Stir in fresh cilantro leaves and lime juice.
7. Season with salt to taste.
8. Garnish with lime wedges if desired.

Pro tip: Add a pinch of grated lime zest for extra citrusy flavor.

## Fun Facts

Cilantro Lime Rice is a fragrant and zesty side dish that pairs beautifully with Mexican and Tex-Mex cuisine.

4
servings

170
calories
per
serving

15
minutes

# Black Bean Salad

Black Bean Salad is a refreshing side dish. Black beans are tossed with corn, bell peppers, red onion, and a zesty lime dressing for a vibrant salad.

## Ingredients:

- 2 cans (15 ounces each) black beans, drained and rinsed
- 1 cup corn kernels (fresh, canned, or frozen)
- 1 red bell pepper, diced
- 1/2 red onion, finely chopped
- Juice of 2 limes
- 2 tablespoons olive oil
- 1 teaspoon ground cumin
- Salt and pepper to taste
- Chopped fresh cilantro for garnish (optional)

## Directions

1. In a large bowl, combine black beans, corn kernels, diced red bell pepper, and finely chopped red onion.
2. In a separate small bowl, whisk together lime juice, olive oil, ground cumin, salt, and pepper.
3. Pour the dressing over the bean mixture.
4. Toss until everything is well-coated and combined.
5. Garnish with chopped fresh cilantro if desired.

Pro tip: Add diced avocado for creaminess and extra flavor.

## Fun Facts

Black Bean Salad is a vibrant and nutritious side dish that's packed with color and flavor.

4
servings

120
calories
per
serving

20
minutes

# Grilled Cactus Salad

Grilled Cactus Salad is a unique and healthy side dish. Cactus pads are grilled and combined with tomatoes, onions, and cilantro for a refreshing salad.

## Ingredients:

- 2 cactus pads (nopales), cleaned and sliced into strips
- 2 tomatoes, diced
- 1/2 red onion, finely chopped
- 1/2 cup chopped fresh cilantro
- Juice of 2 limes
- 2 tablespoons olive oil
- Salt and pepper to taste
- Sliced jalapeños for garnish (optional)

## Fun Facts

Grilled Cactus Salad is a healthy and exotic side dish that's a delicacy in Mexican cuisine.

## Directions

1. Preheat a grill or grill pan to medium-high heat.
2. Grill the cleaned and sliced cactus pads until they have grill marks and are tender, about 5-7 minutes per side.
3. Remove the cactus pads from the grill and let them cool.
4. Slice the grilled cactus into smaller pieces.
5. In a large bowl, combine grilled cactus, diced tomatoes, finely chopped red onion, and chopped fresh cilantro.
6. In a separate small bowl, whisk together lime juice, olive oil, salt, and pepper.
7. Pour the dressing over the salad and toss until well-combined.
8. Garnish with sliced jalapeños if desired.

Pro tip: Serve as a taco or tostada topping for a unique twist.

4
servings

120
calories
per
serving

15
minutes

# Jicama Slaw

Jicama Slaw is a crisp and refreshing side dish. Jicama, carrots, and cabbage are tossed in a tangy lime dressing for a crunchy salad.

## Ingredients:

- 1 jicama, peeled and julienned
- 2 carrots, peeled and julienned
- 1/2 small green cabbage, thinly sliced
- 1/4 cup chopped fresh cilantro
- Juice of 2 limes
- 2 tablespoons honey
- 2 tablespoons olive oil
- Salt and pepper to taste
- Chopped fresh mint for garnish (optional)

## Directions

1. In a large bowl, combine julienned jicama, julienned carrots, thinly sliced green cabbage, and chopped fresh cilantro.
2. In a separate small bowl, whisk together lime juice, honey, olive oil, salt, and pepper.
3. Pour the dressing over the slaw mixture.
4. Toss until everything is well-coated and combined.
5. Garnish with chopped fresh mint if desired.

Pro tip: Add a dash of hot sauce for a spicy kick.

## Fun Facts

Jicama Slaw is a crisp and tangy side dish that's perfect for adding a refreshing crunch to your meal.

4
servings

210
calories
per
serving

15
minutes

# Avocado Salad

Avocado Salad is a creamy and healthy side dish. Avocado, tomato, red onion, and cilantro are dressed with lime juice and olive oil for a flavorful salad.

## Ingredients:

- 2 avocados, diced
- 2 tomatoes, diced
- 1/2 red onion, finely chopped
- 1/4 cup chopped fresh cilantro
- Juice of 2 limes
- 2 tablespoons olive oil
- Salt and pepper to taste
- Crumbled queso fresco for garnish (optional)

## Directions

1. In a large bowl, combine diced avocados, diced tomatoes, finely chopped red onion, and chopped fresh cilantro.
2. In a separate small bowl, whisk together lime juice, olive oil, salt, and pepper.
3. Pour the dressing over the salad mixture.
4. Toss until everything is well-coated and combined.
5. Garnish with crumbled queso fresco if desired.

Pro tip: Add sliced jalapeños for a spicy twist.

## Fun Facts

Avocado Salad is a creamy and refreshing side dish that's perfect for avocado lovers.

**8**
servings

**320**
calories
per
serving

**60**
minutes

# Tres Leches Cake

Tres Leches Cake is a decadent dessert. A sponge cake is soaked in three types of milk and topped with whipped cream for a sweet indulgence.

## Ingredients:

- 1 cup all-purpose flour
- 1 1/2 teaspoons baking powder
- 1/2 teaspoon salt
- 4 large eggs
- 1 cup granulated sugar
- 1 teaspoon vanilla extract
- 1/2 cup whole milk
- 1 can (12 ounces) evaporated milk
- 1 can (14 ounces) sweetened condensed milk
- 1 cup heavy cream
- 2 tablespoons powdered sugar
- Fresh fruit for garnish (optional)

## Fun Facts

Tres Leches Cake is a sweet and indulgent dessert that's a beloved treat in Mexican cuisine.

## Directions

1. Preheat the oven to 350°F (175°C). Grease and flour a 9x13-inch baking dish.
2. In a mixing bowl, whisk together all-purpose flour, baking powder, and salt.
3. In a separate bowl, beat eggs until they are light and frothy.
4. Gradually add granulated sugar and vanilla extract to the eggs, and continue beating until the mixture is thick and pale.
5. Gently fold the dry ingredients into the egg mixture.
6. Pour in the whole milk and mix until the batter is smooth.
7. Pour the batter into the prepared baking dish and spread it evenly.
8. Bake in the preheated oven for 30-35 minutes or until a toothpick inserted into the center comes out clean.
9. While the cake is still warm, use a fork to poke holes all over the surface.
10. In a mixing bowl, whisk together evaporated milk, sweetened condensed milk, and heavy cream.
11. Pour the milk mixture over the warm cake, ensuring it soaks in evenly.
12. Cover and refrigerate the cake for at least 4 hours or overnight to allow it to soak.
13. Before serving, whip heavy cream and powdered sugar until stiff peaks form.
14. Spread whipped cream over the cake and garnish with fresh fruit if desired.

Pro tip: Top with a sprinkle of cinnamon for extra flavor.

# Chapter 8:
## Divine Desserts & Drinks

4
servings

220
calories
per
serving

30
minutes

# Churros

Churros are crispy fried dough sticks, dusted with cinnamon sugar. These Spanish treats are popular in Mexican cuisine and perfect for dipping in chocolate sauce.

## Ingredients:

- 1 cup water
- 2 1/2 tablespoons granulated sugar
- 1/2 teaspoon salt
- 2 tablespoons vegetable oil
- 1 cup all-purpose flour
- 2 quarts vegetable oil (for frying)
- 1/2 cup granulated sugar (for coating)
- 1 teaspoon ground cinnamon (for coating)
- Chocolate sauce for dipping (optional)

## Directions

1. In a saucepan, combine water, sugar, salt, and 2 tablespoons of vegetable oil.
2. Bring the mixture to a boil, then remove it from heat.
3. Stir in all-purpose flour until the dough comes together and forms a ball.
4. Heat vegetable oil in a large, deep skillet or Dutch oven to 375°F (190°C).
5. Transfer the churro dough to a piping bag fitted with a star tip.
6. Carefully pipe strips of dough into the hot oil, using scissors or a knife to cut them.
7. Fry until golden brown and crispy, about 2-3 minutes per side.
8. Remove churros from the oil and drain on paper towels.
9. In a shallow dish, combine 1/2 cup granulated sugar and 1 teaspoon ground cinnamon.
10. Roll warm churros in the cinnamon sugar mixture to coat them.
11. Serve with chocolate sauce for dipping if desired.

Pro tip: Enjoy churros while they're warm and fresh!

## Fun Facts

Churros are a beloved dessert in Mexican cuisine, often enjoyed at festivals and fairs. They pair perfectly with a cup of Mexican hot chocolate.

6
servings

290
calories
per
serving

60
minutes

# Flan

Flan is a creamy caramel custard dessert. It features a silky smooth custard topped with a luscious caramel sauce.

## Ingredients:

- 1 cup granulated sugar (for caramel)
- 1 can (14 ounces) sweetened condensed milk
- 1 can (12 ounces) evaporated milk
- 4 large eggs
- 1 teaspoon vanilla extract
- 1/4 teaspoon salt

## Fun Facts

Flan is a delightful and elegant dessert that's often enjoyed on special occasions in Mexican cuisine.

## Directions

1. Preheat your oven to 350°F (175°C).
2. In a saucepan, melt 1 cup of granulated sugar over medium heat, stirring constantly until it turns into a golden-brown caramel.
3. Quickly pour the caramel into the bottom of a baking dish, swirling to coat the bottom evenly.
4. In a mixing bowl, combine sweetened condensed milk, evaporated milk, eggs, vanilla extract, and salt.
5. Whisk until the mixture is smooth and well combined.
6. Pour the custard mixture over the caramel in the baking dish.
7. Cover the dish with aluminum foil.
8. Place the baking dish in a larger pan filled with hot water.
9. Bake in the preheated oven for 50-60 minutes, or until the flan is set but still slightly jiggly in the center.
10. Remove from the oven and let it cool to room temperature.
11. Once cool, refrigerate for at least 4 hours or overnight.
12. To serve, run a knife around the edge of the dish to loosen the flan.
13. Place a serving plate on top of the dish and invert it to release the flan with the caramel sauce on top.

Pro tip: Garnish with fresh berries or mint leaves for an elegant touch.

4
servings

240
calories
per
serving

15
minutes

# Mexican Hot Chocolate

Mexican Hot Chocolate is a rich and comforting drink. It's made with dark chocolate, cinnamon, and a hint of chili for a warming treat.

## Ingredients:

- 4 cups whole milk
- 4 ounces dark chocolate, finely chopped
- 2 tablespoons granulated sugar (adjust to taste)
- 1 teaspoon ground cinnamon
- 1/4 teaspoon chili powder (adjust to taste)
- Whipped cream and cinnamon sticks for garnish (optional)

## Directions

1. In a saucepan, heat whole milk over medium heat until it's hot but not boiling.
2. Add finely chopped dark chocolate to the milk.
3. Whisk continuously until the chocolate is melted and the mixture is smooth.
4. Stir in granulated sugar, ground cinnamon, and chili powder.
5. Continue to cook and whisk until the hot chocolate is heated through.
6. Taste and adjust the sweetness and spiciness to your liking by adding more sugar or chili powder if needed.
7. Pour the Mexican hot chocolate into mugs.
8. Top with whipped cream and garnish with cinnamon sticks if desired.

Pro tip: Serve with churros for a classic pairing.

## Fun Facts

Mexican Hot Chocolate is a cozy and indulgent drink, perfect for warming up on chilly evenings.

4
servings

180
calories
per
serving

10
minutes

# Horchata

Horchata is a creamy and refreshing rice milk drink. It's flavored with cinnamon and vanilla for a delightful and cooling beverage.

## Ingredients:

- 1 cup long-grain white rice, rinsed
- 4 cups water
- 1 cinnamon stick
- 1/2 cup granulated sugar (adjust to taste)
- 1 teaspoon vanilla extract
- Ground cinnamon for garnish (optional)

## Directions

1. In a blender, combine rinsed long-grain white rice, water, and a cinnamon stick.
2. Blend until the mixture is smooth.
3. Strain the rice milk through a fine-mesh sieve or cheesecloth into a pitcher, discarding the solids.
4. Stir in granulated sugar and vanilla extract, adjusting the sweetness to your liking.
5. Chill the horchata in the refrigerator.
6. Before serving, stir the horchata well and pour it into glasses filled with ice.
7. Garnish with a sprinkle of ground cinnamon if desired.

Pro tip: Horchata is a great accompaniment to spicy foods to cool the palate.

## Fun Facts

Horchata is a beloved and cooling beverage enjoyed in Mexican cuisine, particularly with spicy dishes.

2
servings

250
calories
per
serving

10
minutes

# Margarita

Margarita is a classic Mexican cocktail. It's a zesty blend of tequila, lime juice, and orange liqueur, served with a salted rim.

## Ingredients:

- 4 ounces tequila
- 2 ounces fresh lime juice
- 1 ounce orange liqueur (such as Triple Sec or Grand Marnier)
- 1 ounce simple syrup (adjust to taste)
- Salt for rimming the glasses
- Lime wedges for garnish

## Directions

1. Run a lime wedge along the rims of two glasses to wet them.
2. Dip the wet rims into a plate of salt to coat them.
3. In a cocktail shaker, combine tequila, fresh lime juice, orange liqueur, and simple syrup.
4. Fill the shaker with ice and shake vigorously until well chilled.
5. Strain the margarita mixture into the prepared glasses filled with ice.
6. Garnish each glass with a lime wedge.

Pro tip: For a twist, try a flavored margarita by adding fruit puree or using different types of tequila.

## Fun Facts

Margarita is a classic and tangy cocktail that's perfect for celebrating or simply enjoying a refreshing drink.

2
servings

250
calories
per
serving

10
minutes

# Piña Colada

Easy

Piña Colada is a tropical delight. It's a blend of coconut cream, pineapple juice, and rum, served with a garnish of fresh pineapple and a maraschino cherry.

## Ingredients:

- 4 ounces white rum
- 4 ounces pineapple juice
- 2 ounces coconut cream
- 1 cup crushed ice
- Pineapple slices and maraschino cherries for garnish (optional)

## Directions

1. In a blender, combine white rum, pineapple juice, coconut cream, and crushed ice.
2. Blend until the mixture is smooth and creamy.
3. Pour the piña colada into glasses.
4. Garnish with pineapple slices and maraschino cherries if desired.

Pro tip: For a non-alcoholic version, omit the rum and add extra pineapple juice.

## Fun Facts

Piña Colada is a tropical and creamy cocktail that's perfect for sipping by the pool or at the beach.

4
servings

Varies

10
minutes

# Agua Fresca

Agua Fresca is a refreshing fruit drink. It's made by blending fresh fruit with water and a touch of sweetness for a thirst-quenching beverage.

## Ingredients:

- 2 cups fresh fruit (such as watermelon, cantaloupe, or strawberries), cubed
- 4 cups water
- 2-4 tablespoons granulated sugar (adjust to taste)
- Juice of 1 lime (optional)
- Fresh mint leaves for garnish (optional)

## Directions

1. In a blender, combine fresh fruit and water.
2. Blend until the mixture is smooth.
3. Taste and add granulated sugar and lime juice if needed, adjusting to your preferred sweetness.
4. Strain the agua fresca through a fine-mesh sieve into a pitcher, discarding any solids.
5. Chill the drink in the refrigerator.
6. Stir well before serving, as natural fruit juices may settle.
7. Serve in glasses over ice and garnish with fresh mint leaves if desired.

Pro tip: Try different fruit combinations for unique flavors.

## Fun Facts

Agua Fresca is a light and hydrating beverage that showcases the vibrant flavors of fresh fruit.

2
servings

150
calories
per
serving

5
minutes

# Michelada

Michelada is a spicy and savory beer cocktail. It's made with Mexican beer, lime juice, hot sauce, and spices, served with a salted rim and garnished with a lime wedge.

## Ingredients:

- 2 bottles (12 ounces each) Mexican beer (such as lager or pilsner)
- Juice of 2 limes
- 2 teaspoons hot sauce (adjust to taste)
- 1/2 teaspoon Worcestershire sauce
- 1/4 teaspoon soy sauce
- Salt for rimming the glasses
- Lime wedges for garnish (optional)

## Directions

1. Run a lime wedge along the rims of two glasses to wet them.
2. Dip the wet rims into a plate of salt to coat them.
3. In a large glass, combine fresh lime juice, hot sauce, Worcestershire sauce, and soy sauce.
4. Fill the glasses with ice.
5. Pour the Mexican beer into each glass.
6. Stir gently to combine.
7. Garnish each glass with a lime wedge.

Pro tip: Customize the spice level by adjusting the amount of hot sauce.

## Fun Facts

Michelada is a zesty and spicy beer cocktail that's a popular choice for cooling off on a hot day.

2
servings

180
calories
per
serving

5
minutes

# Paloma Cocktail

Paloma Cocktail is a refreshing and citrusy drink. It's made with tequila, grapefruit soda, and lime juice, served with a salted rim and a lime wedge.

## Ingredients:

- 4 ounces tequila
- 8 ounces grapefruit soda (such as Squirt or Jarritos)
- Juice of 1 lime
- Salt for rimming the glasses
- Lime wedges for garnish (optional)

## Directions

1. Run a lime wedge along the rims of two glasses to wet them.
2. Dip the wet rims into a plate of salt to coat them.
3. In each glass, combine tequila, grapefruit soda, and fresh lime juice.
4. Fill the glasses with ice and stir gently to combine.
5. Garnish each glass with a lime wedge.

Pro tip: For a twist, use fresh grapefruit juice and soda water instead of grapefruit soda.

## Fun Facts

Paloma Cocktail is a zesty and effervescent drink that's a popular choice in Mexican cocktail culture.

# Chapter 9:
## Sensational Salsas & Marinades

Varies  Varies  15 minutes

# Al Pastor Marinade

Al Pastor Marinade is a flavor-packed sauce that's perfect for marinating pork. It's a blend of spices, chilies, and pineapple for a sweet and savory profile.

## Ingredients:

- 2 dried ancho chilies, stemmed and seeded
- 2 dried guajillo chilies, stemmed and seeded
- 2 cloves garlic, minced
- 1/2 cup fresh pineapple, diced
- 1/4 cup white vinegar
- 1/4 cup achiote paste
- 1 tablespoon ground cumin
- 1 teaspoon ground cinnamon
- 1 teaspoon dried oregano
- 1/2 teaspoon ground cloves
- 1/2 teaspoon salt
- 1/4 teaspoon black pepper
- 1/4 cup water

## Directions

1. In a dry skillet over medium heat, toast the dried ancho and guajillo chilies for a few seconds on each side until fragrant. Remove from heat.
2. Place the toasted chilies in a bowl of hot water and let them soak for about 15 minutes until they soften.
3. Drain the chilies and transfer them to a blender.
4. Add minced garlic, diced fresh pineapple, white vinegar, achiote paste, ground cumin, ground cinnamon, dried oregano, ground cloves, salt, black pepper, and water to the blender.
5. Blend until the marinade is smooth and well combined.
6. Use the Al Pastor Marinade to marinate pork or your protein of choice for at least 2 hours or overnight in the refrigerator before grilling or roasting.

Pro tip: This marinade is excellent for making Al Pastor tacos.

## Fun Facts

Al Pastor Marinade is a key component of Al Pastor tacos, a beloved street food in Mexico known for its unique flavor combination.

Varies

Varies

10 minutes

# Adobo Marinade

Adobo Marinade is a versatile and spicy sauce that's great for marinating meats, poultry, or seafood.

## Ingredients:

- 3 dried ancho chilies, stemmed and seeded
- 2 cloves garlic, minced
- 1/2 cup white vinegar
- 2 tablespoons ground cumin
- 1 tablespoon dried oregano
- 1 teaspoon smoked paprika
- 1/2 teaspoon ground cinnamon
- 1/2 teaspoon salt
- 1/4 teaspoon black pepper
- 1/4 cup water

## Fun Facts

Adobo Marinade is a classic and versatile sauce used in many Mexican recipes, offering a rich and smoky flavor profile.

## Directions

1. In a dry skillet over medium heat, toast the dried ancho chilies for a few seconds on each side until fragrant. Remove from heat.
2. Place the toasted chilies in a bowl of hot water and let them soak for about 15 minutes until they soften.
3. Drain the chilies and transfer them to a blender.
4. Add minced garlic, white vinegar, ground cumin, dried oregano, smoked paprika, ground cinnamon, salt, black pepper, and water to the blender.
5. Blend until the marinade is smooth and well combined.
6. Use the Adobo Marinade to marinate your choice of meat, poultry, or seafood for at least 30 minutes before grilling, roasting, or pan-searing.

Pro tip: This marinade is a staple in Mexican cuisine and adds depth and flavor to various dishes.

Varies

Varies

10 minutes

# Citrus Chipotle Marinade

Citrus Chipotle Marinade is a zesty and smoky sauce that's perfect for marinating chicken or shrimp.

## Ingredients:

- 3 canned chipotle peppers in adobo sauce
- 2 cloves garlic, minced
- Juice of 2 oranges
- Juice of 2 limes
- 1/4 cup olive oil
- 1 teaspoon ground cumin
- 1/2 teaspoon smoked paprika
- 1/2 teaspoon dried oregano
- 1/2 teaspoon salt
- 1/4 teaspoon black pepper
- Zest of 1 orange (optional)
- Zest of 1 lime (optional)

## Directions

1. In a blender, combine canned chipotle peppers in adobo sauce, minced garlic, orange juice, lime juice, olive oil, ground cumin, smoked paprika, dried oregano, salt, black pepper, and optional orange and lime zest.
2. Blend until the marinade is smooth and well combined.
3. Use the Citrus Chipotle Marinade to marinate chicken or shrimp for at least 30 minutes before grilling or cooking as desired.

Pro tip: This marinade adds a delightful smoky and tangy flavor to your dishes.

## Fun Facts

Citrus Chipotle Marinade is a lively and smoky sauce that brings a burst of flavor to your grilled chicken or shrimp.

Varies | Varies | 10 minutes

# Green Chili Marinade

Green Chili Marinade is a mild and tangy sauce perfect for marinating chicken or pork.

## Ingredients:

- 4 tomatillos, husked and rinsed
- 2 green chilies (such as Anaheim or poblano), roasted, peeled, and seeded
- 2 cloves garlic, minced
- Juice of 2 limes
- 1/4 cup fresh cilantro
- 1 teaspoon ground cumin
- 1/2 teaspoon salt
- 1/4 teaspoon black pepper
- 1/4 cup water

## Directions

1. In a blender, combine husked and rinsed tomatillos, roasted and peeled green chilies, minced garlic, lime juice, fresh cilantro, ground cumin, salt, black pepper, and water.
2. Blend until the marinade is smooth and well combined.
3. Use the Green Chili Marinade to marinate chicken or pork for at least 30 minutes before grilling or cooking as desired.

Pro tip: Roast the green chilies over an open flame or in the oven for a smoky flavor.

## Fun Facts

Green Chili Marinade is a fresh and tangy sauce that's perfect for adding a zing to your grilled chicken or pork dishes.

Varies   Varies   10 minutes

# Cilantro Lime Marinade

Cilantro Lime Marinade is a bright and zesty sauce that's great for marinating chicken or fish.

## Ingredients:

- 1 cup fresh cilantro leaves and stems
- 2 cloves garlic
- Juice of 2 limes
- 1/4 cup olive oil
- 1 teaspoon ground cumin
- 1/2 teaspoon salt
- 1/4 teaspoon black pepper
- 1/4 cup water

## Directions

1. In a blender, combine fresh cilantro leaves and stems, garlic, lime juice, olive oil, ground cumin, salt, black pepper, and water.
2. Blend until the marinade is smooth and well combined.
3. Use the Cilantro Lime Marinade to marinate chicken or fish for at least 30 minutes before grilling or cooking as desired.

Pro tip: This marinade adds a burst of fresh flavor to your dishes.

## Fun Facts

Cilantro Lime Marinade is a vibrant and citrusy sauce that's perfect for enhancing the flavors of chicken or fish.

Varies  Varies  15 minutes

# Tamarind Salsa

Tamarind Salsa is a tangy and sweet sauce that's great for drizzling over grilled meats or seafood.

## Ingredients:

- 1/2 cup tamarind pulp
- 1/4 cup hot water
- 2 tablespoons brown sugar (adjust to taste)
- 1 tablespoon fish sauce
- 1 clove garlic, minced
- 1/2 teaspoon chili flakes (adjust to taste)
- Salt to taste
- Lime wedges for serving (optional)

## Directions

1. In a bowl, combine tamarind pulp and hot water. Let it soak for about 10 minutes to soften.
2. Use your fingers to break up the tamarind pulp and extract the juice. Strain the tamarind juice into another bowl, discarding any solids or seeds.
3. Add brown sugar, fish sauce, minced garlic, chili flakes, and salt to the tamarind juice. Adjust the sweetness and spiciness to your liking.
4. Stir until the ingredients are well combined.
5. Serve the Tamarind Salsa with grilled meats or seafood, along with lime wedges for squeezing.

Pro tip: Tamarind adds a unique sweet and tangy flavor to your dishes.

## Fun Facts

Tamarind Salsa is a distinctive sauce that's popular in Southeast Asian and Mexican cuisines, offering a harmonious blend of flavors.

Varies

Varies

15 minutes

# Salsa Ranchera

Salsa Ranchera is a smoky and spicy sauce that's perfect for adding a kick to your favorite dishes.

## Ingredients:

- 4 dried guajillo chilies, stemmed and seeded
- 1/2 onion, chopped
- 2 cloves garlic, minced
- 1 can (14 ounces) crushed tomatoes
- 1 teaspoon ground cumin
- 1/2 teaspoon dried oregano
- 1/2 teaspoon smoked paprika
- 1/2 teaspoon salt
- 1/4 teaspoon black pepper
- 2 tablespoons vegetable oil

## Fun Facts

Salsa Ranchera is a fiery and flavorful sauce that's perfect for those who love bold and spicy flavors in their dishes.

## Directions

1. In a dry skillet over medium heat, toast the dried guajillo chilies for a few seconds on each side until fragrant. Remove from heat.
2. Place the toasted chilies in a bowl of hot water and let them soak for about 15 minutes until they soften.
3. Drain the chilies and transfer them to a blender.
4. Add chopped onion, minced garlic, crushed tomatoes, ground cumin, dried oregano, smoked paprika, salt, and black pepper to the blender.
5. Blend until the salsa is smooth.
6. In a saucepan, heat vegetable oil over medium heat.
7. Carefully pour the blended salsa into the hot oil. Be cautious, as it may splatter.
8. Cook the salsa for about 10 minutes, stirring occasionally, until it thickens and deepens in color.
9. Taste and adjust the seasoning as needed.
10. Serve Salsa Ranchera with your favorite dishes.

Pro tip: This salsa adds a smoky and spicy kick to your tacos and grilled meats.

Varies | Varies | 10 minutes

# Salsa Negra

Salsa Negra is a smoky and intense sauce that's great for drizzling over tacos or grilled meats.

## Ingredients:

- 6 dried arbol chilies, stemmed
- 4 cloves garlic, peeled
- 1/4 cup vegetable oil
- 2 tablespoons soy sauce
- 1 tablespoon brown sugar
- 1/2 teaspoon salt
- 1/4 teaspoon black pepper
- 1/4 teaspoon dried oregano

## Fun Facts

Salsa Negra is a smoky and intense sauce that adds a bold kick to your dishes, perfect for those who crave spicy flavors.

## Directions

1. In a dry skillet over medium heat, toast the dried arbol chilies for a few seconds on each side until fragrant. Remove from heat.
2. Place the toasted chilies in a bowl of hot water and let them soak for about 15 minutes until they soften.
3. Drain the chilies and transfer them to a blender.
4. Add peeled garlic cloves, vegetable oil, soy sauce, brown sugar, salt, black pepper, and dried oregano to the blender.
5. Blend until the salsa is smooth and well combined.
6. Serve Salsa Negra with tacos, grilled meats, or any dish that craves a smoky kick.

Pro tip: This salsa is bold and intense, so use it sparingly if you prefer milder flavors.

Varies
Varies
10 minutes

# Tomatillo Avocado Salsa

Tomatillo Avocado Salsa is a creamy and tangy sauce that's great for dipping chips or topping tacos.

## Ingredients:

- 4 tomatillos, husked and rinsed
- 1 avocado, peeled and pitted
- 1/2 onion, chopped
- 2 cloves garlic, minced
- 1/2 cup fresh cilantro
- Juice of 2 limes
- 1/2 teaspoon salt
- 1/4 teaspoon black pepper
- 1/4 teaspoon cayenne pepper (optional)
- 1/4 cup water

## Directions

1. In a blender, combine husked and rinsed tomatillos, peeled and pitted avocado, chopped onion, minced garlic, fresh cilantro, lime juice, salt, black pepper, and optional cayenne pepper for heat.
2. Blend until the salsa is creamy and well combined.
3. Add water as needed to achieve your desired consistency.
4. Taste and adjust the seasoning to your liking.
5. Serve Tomatillo Avocado Salsa as a dip for chips or a topping for tacos and grilled meats.

Pro tip: This salsa is creamy and tangy, with a hint of heat from the optional cayenne pepper.

## Fun Facts

Tomatillo Avocado Salsa is a creamy and tangy sauce that adds a refreshing twist to your favorite Mexican dishes.

Varies   Varies   15 minutes

# Roasted Garlic Salsa

Roasted Garlic Salsa is a rich and flavorful sauce that's perfect for drizzling over grilled meats.

## Ingredients:

- 6 cloves garlic, peeled
- 4 Roma tomatoes
- 2 dried guajillo chilies, stemmed and seeded
- 1/2 onion, chopped
- 1/4 cup fresh cilantro
- Juice of 2 limes
- 1 teaspoon ground cumin
- 1/2 teaspoon salt
- 1/4 teaspoon black pepper
- 1/4 teaspoon dried oregano

## Fun Facts

Roasted Garlic Salsa is a flavorful and smoky sauce that's perfect for enhancing the taste of grilled meats and tacos.

## Directions

1. Preheat your oven's broiler.
2. Place peeled garlic cloves, Roma tomatoes, and dried guajillo chilies on a baking sheet.
3. Broil the ingredients for about 5-7 minutes, turning them occasionally, until they are charred and blistered.
4. Remove from the oven and let them cool slightly.
5. In a blender, combine the roasted garlic cloves, peeled tomatoes, toasted dried guajillo chilies, chopped onion, fresh cilantro, lime juice, ground cumin, salt, black pepper, and dried oregano.
6. Blend until the salsa is smooth and well combined.
7. Serve Roasted Garlic Salsa with grilled meats, tacos, or as a dip for tortilla chips.

Pro tip: Roasting the garlic and tomatoes adds a rich and smoky flavor to the salsa.

# Chapter 10:
## Mexican Breakfast Favorites

4 servings

Varies

30 minutes

Easy

# Chilaquiles

Chilaquiles are a delightful breakfast dish featuring crispy tortilla chips smothered in salsa and topped with eggs and cheese.

## Ingredients:

- 1 bag (10 ounces) tortilla chips
- 2 cups red or green salsa
- 4 eggs
- 1 cup shredded cheese (such as Monterey Jack or cheddar)
- 1/2 cup sour cream (optional)
- 1/4 cup fresh cilantro, chopped
- 1/4 cup red onion, finely chopped
- 1/4 cup queso fresco or feta cheese, crumbled
- Avocado slices for garnish (optional)

## Fun Facts

Chilaquiles are a classic Mexican breakfast dish that's known for its perfect combination of crispy and saucy textures, making it a beloved morning treat.

## Directions

1. In a large skillet, heat the salsa over medium heat until it simmers.
2. Add the tortilla chips to the skillet and gently toss to coat them with the salsa. Cook for about 5 minutes, stirring occasionally, until the chips soften slightly but remain crispy.
3. Create small wells in the chip mixture and crack an egg into each well.
4. Sprinkle shredded cheese over the top of the chips and eggs.
5. Cover the skillet and cook for about 5-7 minutes, or until the eggs are cooked to your desired level of doneness and the cheese is melted.
6. Remove from heat and garnish with sour cream, fresh cilantro, chopped red onion, crumbled queso fresco, and avocado slices if desired.
7. Serve immediately.

Pro tip: Chilaquiles are a great way to use up leftover tortilla chips and salsa.

**4 servings** | **Varies** kcal | **20 minutes**

# Huevos Rancheros

Huevos Rancheros is a hearty breakfast featuring fried eggs on corn tortillas smothered in tomato-chili sauce.

## Ingredients:

- 4 corn tortillas
- 4 eggs
- 2 cups tomato sauce
- 2 cloves garlic, minced
- 1/2 onion, chopped
- 1 jalapeño pepper, chopped (remove seeds for milder heat)
- 1 teaspoon ground cumin
- 1/2 teaspoon chili powder
- 1/2 teaspoon paprika
- Salt and pepper to taste
- 1/4 cup fresh cilantro, chopped
- 1/4 cup queso fresco or feta cheese, crumbled
- Lime wedges for garnish (optional)

## Fun Facts

Huevos Rancheros is a classic Mexican breakfast dish known for its hearty and bold flavors, making it a satisfying start to the day.

## Directions

1. In a saucepan, heat 2 tablespoons of oil over medium heat. Add minced garlic and chopped onion, and sauté until they become fragrant and the onion is translucent.
2. Stir in the chopped jalapeño pepper, ground cumin, chili powder, paprika, salt, and pepper. Cook for an additional 2-3 minutes.
3. Pour in the tomato sauce and simmer for about 10 minutes, allowing the flavors to meld.
4. While the sauce simmers, heat the remaining oil in a separate skillet over medium-high heat. Add corn tortillas, one at a time, and cook for about 1-2 minutes per side until they become slightly crispy.
5. In the same skillet, fry the eggs to your desired level of doneness.
6. To serve, place a corn tortilla on each plate, spoon the tomato-chili sauce over it, and top with a fried egg.
7. Garnish with fresh cilantro, crumbled queso fresco, and lime wedges if desired.
8. Serve immediately.

Pro tip: Huevos Rancheros is perfect for breakfast or brunch, and it's sure to satisfy your cravings for savory and spicy flavors.

4
servings

Varies

25
minutes

# Breakfast Burrito

Breakfast Burritos are a convenient morning meal, featuring scrambled eggs, breakfast meats, and toppings wrapped in a tortilla.

## Ingredients:

- 4 large flour tortillas
- 8 large eggs
- 1/2 cup cooked bacon or sausage, crumbled
- 1/2 cup shredded cheese (such as cheddar or pepper jack)
- 1/2 cup bell peppers, diced
- 1/2 cup onions, diced
- 1/4 cup fresh cilantro, chopped
- 1/4 cup salsa
- Salt and pepper to taste
- Cooking oil for sautéing

## Directions

1. In a skillet, heat a bit of oil over medium heat. Add diced onions and bell peppers and sauté until they become tender, about 3-4 minutes.
2. In a bowl, whisk the eggs and season with salt and pepper.
3. Push the sautéed onions and peppers to one side of the skillet and add the eggs to the other side. Scramble the eggs until they are just set.
4. Assemble the burritos: Lay out each tortilla, and fill them with scrambled eggs, crumbled bacon or sausage, shredded cheese, fresh cilantro, and salsa.
5. Fold the sides of the tortilla over the filling and roll it up tightly to form a burrito.
6. In the same skillet used for the eggs, heat each burrito seam-side down for about 1-2 minutes, or until they are golden brown and crispy.
7. Serve the Breakfast Burritos hot.

Pro tip: Customize your Breakfast Burrito with your favorite ingredients like avocado, beans, or hot sauce.

## Fun Facts

Breakfast Burritos are a versatile morning option that lets you create your perfect combination of flavors and textures.

4
servings

Varies

20
minutes

Breakfast Tacos are a quick and satisfying morning treat, featuring scrambled eggs, toppings, and a warm tortilla.

# Breakfast Tacos

## Ingredients:

- 4 small flour or corn tortillas
- 6 large eggs
- 1/2 cup cooked chorizo or breakfast sausage, crumbled
- 1/2 cup shredded cheese (such as Monterey Jack or queso fresco)
- 1/4 cup fresh salsa
- 1/4 cup fresh cilantro, chopped
- Salt and pepper to taste
- Cooking oil for sautéing

## Fun Facts

Breakfast Tacos are a speedy and flavorful way to start your day with a satisfying breakfast.

## Directions

1. In a skillet, heat a bit of oil over medium heat. Add crumbled chorizo or breakfast sausage and cook until browned and cooked through, breaking it apart as it cooks. Remove from the skillet and set aside.
2. In a bowl, whisk the eggs and season with salt and pepper.
3. In the same skillet, heat a bit more oil if needed, and pour in the whisked eggs. Scramble the eggs until they are just set.
4. Assemble the tacos: Warm the tortillas in the skillet or microwave. Fill each tortilla with scrambled eggs, cooked chorizo or sausage, shredded cheese, fresh salsa, and chopped cilantro.
5. Serve the Breakfast Tacos hot.

Pro tip: Breakfast Tacos are highly customizable, so feel free to add avocado, jalapeños, or hot sauce to suit your taste.

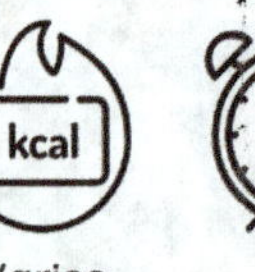

4
servings

Varies

35
minutes

# Breakfast Enchiladas

Breakfast Enchiladas are a delicious morning indulgence, featuring tortillas stuffed with scrambled eggs and smothered in sauce.

## Ingredients:

- 8 small corn tortillas
- 6 large eggs
- 1/2 cup cooked chorizo or breakfast sausage, crumbled
- 1/2 cup shredded cheese (such as cheddar or pepper jack)
- 2 cups red or green enchilada sauce
- 1/4 cup fresh cilantro, chopped
- Salt and pepper to taste
- Cooking oil for sautéing

## Fun Facts

Breakfast Enchiladas are a delightful morning indulgence that combines the comforting flavors of enchiladas with scrambled eggs.

## Directions

1. In a skillet, heat a bit of oil over medium heat. Add crumbled chorizo or breakfast sausage and cook until browned and cooked through. Remove from the skillet and set aside.
2. In a bowl, whisk the eggs and season with salt and pepper.
3. In the same skillet, heat a bit more oil if needed, and pour in the whisked eggs. Scramble the eggs until they are just set.
4. Warm the corn tortillas in the skillet or microwave.
5. Assemble the enchiladas: Pour a small amount of enchilada sauce into the bottom of a baking dish to prevent sticking. Fill each tortilla with scrambled eggs, cooked chorizo or sausage, and shredded cheese. Roll up the tortillas and place them seam-side down in the baking dish.
6. Pour the remaining enchilada sauce over the top of the enchiladas.
7. Bake in a preheated oven at 350°F (175°C) for about 15-20 minutes, or until the enchiladas are heated through and the sauce is bubbly.
8. Garnish with fresh cilantro.
9. Serve the Breakfast Enchiladas hot.

Pro tip: These enchiladas are perfect for brunch gatherings and can be made ahead of time.

4
servings

Varies

20
minutes

# Breakfast Quesadilla

Breakfast Quesadillas are a quick and savory morning option, featuring eggs, cheese, and optional fillings in a tortilla.

## Ingredients:

- 4 large flour tortillas
- 6 large eggs
- 1 cup shredded cheese (such as cheddar or pepper jack)
- 1/2 cup cooked bacon or sausage, crumbled (optional)
- 1/2 cup bell peppers, diced
- 1/4 cup onions, diced
- 1/4 cup fresh salsa
- Salt and pepper to taste
- Cooking oil for sautéing

## Directions

1. In a skillet, heat a bit of oil over medium heat. Add diced onions and bell peppers and sauté until they become tender, about 3-4 minutes.
2. In a bowl, whisk the eggs and season with salt and pepper.
3. In the same skillet, heat a bit more oil if needed, and pour in the whisked eggs. Scramble the eggs until they are just set.
4. Assemble the quesadillas: Lay out each tortilla, and sprinkle shredded cheese over half of each tortilla. Add cooked bacon or sausage (if using), sautéed onions and bell peppers, and fresh salsa on top of the cheese.
5. Fold the other half of each tortilla over the filling to create a half-moon shape.
6. In the same skillet used for the eggs, heat each quesadilla for about 2-3 minutes per side until they become golden brown and the cheese is melted.
7. Serve the Breakfast Quesadillas hot.

Pro tip: Feel free to customize your Breakfast Quesadilla with your favorite breakfast ingredients like avocado or jalapeños.

## Fun Facts

Breakfast Quesadillas are a savory and satisfying morning option that's ready in no time, making them perfect for busy mornings.

4
servings

Varies

30
minutes

# Breakfast Skillet

Breakfast Skillet is a one-pan wonder, combining eggs, potatoes, and breakfast meats in a delicious morning feast.

## Ingredients:

- 4 large eggs
- 2 cups diced potatoes (precooked, such as leftover roasted or boiled potatoes)
- 1/2 cup diced onion
- 1/2 cup diced bell peppers
- 1/2 cup diced cooked bacon or sausage
- 1/2 cup shredded cheese (such as cheddar or Monterey Jack)
- 2 tablespoons cooking oil
- Salt and pepper to taste
- Fresh herbs for garnish (optional)

## Fun Facts

Breakfast Skillet is a hearty and satisfying one-pan breakfast dish that's perfect for sharing with friends and family.

## Directions

1. In a large ovenproof skillet, heat cooking oil over medium heat.
2. Add diced onions and bell peppers and sauté until they become tender, about 3-4 minutes.
3. Add the diced potatoes to the skillet and cook, stirring occasionally, until they are golden brown and crispy.
4. Stir in the cooked bacon or sausage.
5. Create small wells in the potato mixture and crack an egg into each well.
6. Sprinkle shredded cheese over the top of the skillet.
7. Transfer the skillet to a preheated oven at 350°F (175°C) and bake for about 10-12 minutes, or until the eggs are cooked to your desired level of doneness and the cheese is melted and bubbly.
8. Garnish with fresh herbs if desired.
9. Serve the Breakfast Skillet hot directly from the skillet.

Pro tip: You can add diced tomatoes or hot sauce for extra flavor and a touch of heat.

2
servings

Varies

15
minutes

# Mexican Omelette

Mexican Omelette is a fluffy and flavorful breakfast featuring eggs, peppers, onions, and cheese.

## Ingredients:

- 4 large eggs
- 1/4 cup diced bell peppers
- 1/4 cup diced onions
- 1/4 cup shredded cheese (such as cheddar or pepper jack)
- 2 tablespoons butter
- Salt and pepper to taste
- Fresh salsa or avocado for garnish (optional)

## Fun Facts

Mexican Omelette is a quick and fluffy breakfast option that's packed with vibrant Mexican flavors.

## Directions

1. In a bowl, whisk the eggs and season with salt and pepper.
2. In a non-stick skillet, melt 1 tablespoon of butter over medium heat.
3. Add diced bell peppers and onions to the skillet and sauté until they become tender, about 3-4 minutes.
4. Pour the whisked eggs into the skillet with the sautéed vegetables.
5. Allow the eggs to cook without stirring for a few minutes until they start to set.
6. Sprinkle shredded cheese evenly over one half of the omelette.
7. Carefully fold the other half of the omelette over the cheese.
8. Cook for another 2-3 minutes until the cheese is melted and the omelette is cooked through.
9. Slide the Mexican Omelette onto a plate and garnish with fresh salsa or avocado if desired.
10. Serve immediately.

Pro tip: You can add diced tomatoes, jalapeños, or cooked bacon for extra flavor.

4
servings

Varies

25
minutes

# Mexican Breakfast Pizza

Mexican Breakfast Pizza is a fun morning twist on pizza, featuring eggs, salsa, cheese, and optional toppings on a pizza crust.

## Ingredients:

- 1 pre-made pizza crust (store-bought or homemade)
- 4 large eggs
- 1/2 cup salsa
- 1 cup shredded cheese (such as Monterey Jack or cheddar)
- 1/2 cup cooked chorizo or breakfast sausage, crumbled (optional)
- 1/4 cup diced bell peppers
- 1/4 cup diced onions
- 1/4 cup fresh cilantro, chopped
- Salt and pepper to taste
- Cooking oil for sautéing (if needed)

## Directions

1. Preheat your oven according to the pizza crust package instructions.
2. In a skillet, heat a bit of oil over medium heat. If you're using cooked chorizo or breakfast sausage, sauté it until browned and cooked through. Remove from the skillet and set aside.
3. In the same skillet, sauté diced bell peppers and onions until they become tender, about 3-4 minutes.
4. Roll out the pizza crust onto a baking sheet or pizza stone.
5. Spread salsa evenly over the pizza crust.
6. Sprinkle shredded cheese over the salsa.
7. If you're using cooked chorizo or sausage, distribute it evenly over the cheese.
8. Create small wells on the pizza and crack an egg into each well.
9. Bake the Mexican Breakfast Pizza in the preheated oven according to the pizza crust package instructions, or until the eggs are cooked to your desired level of doneness and the crust is golden brown.
10. Remove from the oven and garnish with fresh cilantro.
11. Slice and serve hot.

Pro tip: Customize your Mexican Breakfast Pizza with your favorite breakfast ingredients like avocado or jalapeños.

## Fun Facts

Mexican Breakfast Pizza is a creative and delicious way to enjoy pizza for breakfast, combining classic pizza elements with morning flavors.

**2**
servings

**Varies**

**15**
minutes

# Mexican Breakfast Bowl

Mexican Breakfast Bowl is a satisfying morning dish, featuring a combination of eggs, beans, and toppings in a bowl.

## Ingredients:

- 4 large eggs
- 1 cup cooked black beans
- 1 cup cooked brown rice
- 1/2 cup diced tomatoes
- 1/4 cup diced onions
- 1/4 cup fresh salsa
- 1/4 cup fresh cilantro, chopped
- Salt and pepper to taste
- Avocado slices for garnish (optional)

## Directions

1. In a bowl, whisk the eggs and season with salt and pepper.
2. In a skillet, heat a bit of oil over medium heat. Pour in the whisked eggs and scramble them until they are just set.
3. In a serving bowl, assemble the Mexican Breakfast Bowl: Start with a base of cooked brown rice, and top it with scrambled eggs, cooked black beans, diced tomatoes, diced onions, and fresh salsa.
4. Garnish with fresh cilantro and avocado slices if desired.
5. Serve the Mexican Breakfast Bowl hot.

Pro tip: You can add hot sauce or sour cream for extra flavor and creaminess.

## Fun Facts

Mexican Breakfast Bowl is a wholesome and customizable morning option that's ready in a flash, making it a great choice for busy mornings.

# Chapter 11:
## Party Drinks & Cocktails

1 cocktail | 200-250 | 10 minutes

# Margarita

The Margarita is a classic cocktail known for its tangy and refreshing combination of tequila, lime juice, and orange liqueur.

## Ingredients:

- 2 oz (60 ml) tequila
- 1 oz (30 ml) orange liqueur (such as triple sec or Cointreau)
- 1 oz (30 ml) freshly squeezed lime juice
- 1/2 oz (15 ml) simple syrup (adjust to taste)
- Ice
- Salt (for rimming the glass, optional)
- Lime wheel or wedge for garnish

## Directions

1. If desired, rim the edge of a chilled margarita glass with salt. To do this, rub the rim with a lime wedge, then dip it in a shallow dish of salt.
2. Fill a cocktail shaker with ice.
3. Add the tequila, orange liqueur, freshly squeezed lime juice, and simple syrup to the shaker.
4. Shake vigorously for about 15-20 seconds until well chilled.
5. Strain the Margarita mixture into the prepared glass filled with ice.
6. Garnish with a lime wheel or wedge.
7. Serve immediately and enjoy your Margarita!

Pro tip: For a fun twist, try different fruit juices like mango or blood orange to create flavored Margaritas.

## Fun Facts

The Margarita is a timeless cocktail that brings together the zing of lime and the smoothness of tequila in a perfect harmony of flavors.

1 cocktail    250-300    10 minutes

Easy

# Piña Colada

The Piña Colada is a tropical delight, blending coconut cream, pineapple juice, and rum into a creamy and refreshing drink.

## Ingredients:

- 2 oz (60 ml) white rum
- 2 oz (60 ml) coconut cream
- 3 oz (90 ml) pineapple juice
- 1 cup crushed ice
- Pineapple wedge and maraschino cherry for garnish (optional)

## Directions

1. In a blender, combine white rum, coconut cream, pineapple juice, and crushed ice.
2. Blend until the mixture is smooth and creamy.
3. Pour the Piña Colada into a chilled glass.
4. Garnish with a pineapple wedge and a maraschino cherry if desired.
5. Insert a straw and enjoy your tropical Piña Colada!

Pro tip: You can adjust the amount of coconut cream to achieve your desired level of creaminess.

## Fun Facts

The Piña Colada is like a sip of paradise with its creamy coconut and sweet pineapple flavors. It's the perfect beachside cocktail.

4
servings

Varies

10
minutes

# Agua Fresca

Agua Fresca is a refreshing non-alcoholic drink made from blended fruit, water, and a touch of sweetness.

## Ingredients:

- 4 cups ripe fruit (such as watermelon, cantaloupe, or mango), peeled and diced
- 4 cups water
- 1/4 cup granulated sugar (adjust to taste)
- Fresh lime juice (optional)
- Ice

## Directions

1. Place the diced fruit and water in a blender.
2. Add granulated sugar to the blender. You can adjust the amount of sugar depending on the sweetness of the fruit and your preference.
3. Blend until the mixture is smooth.
4. Taste the Agua Fresca and adjust the sweetness by adding more sugar if needed or a squeeze of fresh lime juice for extra zing.
5. If desired, strain the Agua Fresca through a fine-mesh sieve to remove any pulp or seeds.
6. Serve the Agua Fresca over ice and garnish with fresh fruit slices if desired.
7. Enjoy the refreshing taste of Agua Fresca on a hot day!

Pro tip: Experiment with different fruits and even herbs like mint or basil to create unique Agua Fresca flavors.

## Fun Facts

Agua Fresca is a delightful and hydrating drink that celebrates the natural sweetness of fresh fruit. It's a popular choice in Mexican cuisine.

1 cocktail | Varies | 5 minutes

# Michelada

The Michelada is a spicy and savory beer cocktail with a zesty blend of tomato juice, lime, and hot sauce.

## Ingredients:

- 1 light Mexican beer (such as Corona or Modelo)
- 1/4 cup tomato juice
- 1/2 lime, freshly squeezed
- 2-3 dashes hot sauce (adjust to taste)
- 1 pinch salt (optional)
- Ice
- Tajín or chili powder for rimming the glass (optional)
- Lime wedge for garnish

## Fun Facts

The Michelada is a popular Mexican beer cocktail that's perfect for those who enjoy a hint of spice and tang in their drinks.

## Directions

1. If desired, rim the edge of a chilled beer glass with Tajín or chili powder. To do this, rub the rim with a lime wedge, then dip it in a shallow dish of Tajín or chili powder.
2. Fill the glass with ice.
3. Squeeze the juice of half a lime into the glass.
4. Add hot sauce and a pinch of salt (if using) to the glass.
5. Pour in the tomato juice and stir the mixture gently to combine.
6. Open the Mexican beer and pour it into the glass, pouring slowly to avoid excessive foam.
7. Give it a gentle stir.
8. Garnish with a lime wedge.
9. Serve your Michelada immediately and enjoy its bold flavors.

Pro tip: Customize your Michelada with additional hot sauce, Worcestershire sauce, or even a splash of clamato juice for extra depth of flavor.

1 cocktail

Varies

5 minutes

# Paloma Cocktail

The Paloma Cocktail is a light and citrusy drink made with tequila and grapefruit soda, perfect for a refreshing sip.

## Ingredients:

- 2 oz (60 ml) tequila
- 1/2 oz (15 ml) lime juice
- 1/2 oz (15 ml) simple syrup (adjust to taste)
- Grapefruit soda (such as Squirt or Jarritos)
- Ice
- Lime wheel for garnish (optional)
- Salt or Tajín for rimming the glass (optional)

## Fun Facts

The Paloma Cocktail is a popular Mexican drink that's light, refreshing, and perfect for warm weather. Its citrusy notes make it a delightful choice.

## Directions

1. If desired, rim the edge of a chilled highball glass with salt or Tajín. To do this, rub the rim with a lime wedge, then dip it in a shallow dish of salt or Tajín.
2. Fill the glass with ice.
3. In the glass, combine tequila, lime juice, and simple syrup. Stir to mix well.
4. Top off the mixture with grapefruit soda to your desired level of sweetness, usually about 2-3 ounces.
5. Give it a gentle stir.
6. Garnish with a lime wheel if desired.
7. Serve your Paloma Cocktail and savor its bright and bubbly flavors.

Pro tip: You can adjust the sweetness by adding more or less simple syrup and grapefruit soda according to your taste.

1 cocktail    200-250    10 minutes

# Mezcal Margarita

The Mezcal Margarita is a smoky twist on the classic Margarita, featuring mezcal instead of traditional tequila.

## Ingredients:

- 2 oz (60 ml) mezcal
- 1 oz (30 ml) orange liqueur (such as triple sec or Cointreau)
- 1 oz (30 ml) freshly squeezed lime juice
- 1/2 oz (15 ml) simple syrup (adjust to taste)
- Ice
- Salt (for rimming the glass, optional)
- Lime wheel or wedge for garnish

## Fun Facts

The Mezcal Margarita is a smoky and sophisticated take on the classic Margarita, perfect for those who appreciate bold flavors.

## Directions

1. If desired, rim the edge of a chilled margarita glass with salt. To do this, rub the rim with a lime wedge, then dip it in a shallow dish of salt.
2. Fill a cocktail shaker with ice.
3. Add the mezcal, orange liqueur, freshly squeezed lime juice, and simple syrup to the shaker.
4. Shake vigorously for about 15-20 seconds until well chilled.
5. Strain the Mezcal Margarita mixture into the prepared glass filled with ice.
6. Garnish with a lime wheel or wedge.
7. Serve immediately and enjoy your Mezcal Margarita!

Pro tip: Mezcal adds a smoky depth to this cocktail, making it a unique and flavorful choice for Margarita enthusiasts.

1 cocktail

Varies

5 minutes

# Mexican Mule

The Mexican Mule is a spicy and zesty twist on the Moscow Mule, featuring tequila, lime juice, and ginger beer.

## Ingredients:

- 2 oz (60 ml) tequila
- 1/2 oz (15 ml) lime juice
- Ginger beer
- Ice
- Lime wheel or wedge for garnish

## Directions

1. Fill a copper mule mug or a highball glass with ice.
2. Add tequila and lime juice to the glass.
3. Top off the mixture with ginger beer, leaving some space at the top.
4. Give it a gentle stir.
5. Garnish with a lime wheel or wedge.
6. Serve your Mexican Mule and enjoy the lively combination of flavors.

Pro tip: Adjust the level of spice by using regular or spicy ginger beer. You can also add a slice of fresh ginger for extra kick.

## Fun Facts

The Mexican Mule is a spicy and effervescent cocktail that's perfect for those who enjoy the zesty kick of ginger with a tequila twist.

1 cocktail    Varies    5 minutes

# Tequila Sunrise

The Tequila Sunrise is a visually stunning cocktail with layers of orange juice, grenadine, and tequila.

## Ingredients:

- 2 oz (60 ml) tequila
- 4 oz (120 ml) orange juice
- 1/2 oz (15 ml) grenadine syrup
- Ice
- Orange slice and maraschino cherry for garnish (optional)

## Directions

1. Fill a highball glass with ice.
2. Pour the tequila and orange juice into the glass. Stir to mix well.
3. Slowly pour the grenadine syrup over the back of a spoon or by drizzling it down the side of the glass. It will settle at the bottom and create a beautiful sunrise effect.
4. Garnish with an orange slice and a maraschino cherry if desired.
5. Serve your Tequila Sunrise and savor its vibrant layers of flavor.

Pro tip: The key to the sunrise effect is to pour the grenadine slowly and avoid stirring after adding it.

## Fun Facts

The Tequila Sunrise is a visually striking cocktail that captures the essence of a beautiful sunrise with its vibrant layers of flavor.

**4 servings**

**Varies**

**5 minutes**

# Horchata

Horchata is a creamy and sweet rice milk beverage infused with cinnamon and vanilla, perfect for cooling off on a hot day.

## Ingredients:

- 1 cup long-grain white rice
- 4 cups water
- 1 cinnamon stick
- 1/2 cup granulated sugar (adjust to taste)
- 1 teaspoon vanilla extract
- Ice
- Ground cinnamon for garnish (optional)

## Directions

1. Rinse the rice under cold water until the water runs clear.
2. In a blender, combine the rinsed rice, water, and cinnamon stick. Blend until the rice is broken into fine particles.
3. Strain the mixture through a fine-mesh sieve or cheesecloth into a pitcher, discarding any solids.
4. Stir in granulated sugar and vanilla extract until the sugar is dissolved.
5. Chill the Horchata in the refrigerator until cold.
6. Serve Horchata over ice and garnish with a sprinkle of ground cinnamon if desired.
7. Enjoy the creamy and comforting taste of Horchata!

Pro tip: You can adjust the sweetness and cinnamon flavor to your liking.

## Fun Facts

Horchata is a beloved Mexican beverage known for its creamy texture and comforting flavors of cinnamon and vanilla. It's perfect for sipping on a warm day.

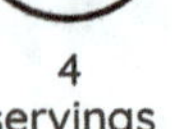

**4 servings** | **Varies** | **10 minutes**

# Mexican Sangria

Mexican Sangria is a delightful twist on the classic Spanish drink, featuring red wine, citrus, and a hint of tequila.

## Ingredients:

- 1 bottle (750 ml) red wine (such as Merlot or Cabernet Sauvignon)
- 1/2 cup tequila
- 1/4 cup orange liqueur (such as triple sec or Cointreau)
- 1/4 cup granulated sugar (adjust to taste)
- 1 orange, sliced
- 1 lemon, sliced
- 1 lime, sliced
- 1 apple, diced
- 1 cup club soda (optional)
- Ice
- Fresh berries for garnish (optional)

## Directions

1. In a large pitcher, combine red wine, tequila, orange liqueur, and granulated sugar. Stir until the sugar is dissolved.
2. Add sliced oranges, lemons, limes, and diced apple to the pitcher.
3. Chill the Mexican Sangria in the refrigerator for at least an hour to let the flavors meld.
4. If desired, add club soda just before serving to add a touch of effervescence.
5. Serve the Sangria over ice and garnish with fresh berries if desired.
6. Enjoy your Mexican Sangria, a fruity and spirited drink perfect for gatherings.

## Fun Facts

Mexican Sangria is a vibrant and fruity drink with a Mexican twist, making it a wonderful choice for celebrations and gatherings.

# We have a small favor to ask

Dear Fellow Lovers of Mexican Fiesta,

As we come to the final pages of our culinary exploration through the "Mexican Fiesta with 5 Ingredients" cookbook, we are overwhelmed with gratitude for sharing this vibrant journey with you. Mexican cuisine is a symphony of flavors, and it has been our pleasure to be your guide in creating simple and satisfying dishes with just five ingredients.

We hope these recipes have allowed you to savor the joy of Mexican flavors, transporting you to bustling street markets, family gatherings, and the heart of Mexico's rich culinary traditions. Mexican cuisine is a celebration of life, and we have strived to capture that spirit in every dish.

Now, we have a humble request for you, our esteemed readers. Reviews are a lifeline for any cookbook, and they are particularly elusive for small, independent publishers like us. If you could spare a moment to pen down a review, assign a star rating, and perhaps share a brief sentence or two about your culinary journey, it would truly mean the world to us.

Each review you provide is a gift we cherish. We read and appreciate every single one. Your insights, your praises, your constructive feedback – they all inspire us as we continue our culinary voyage to bring the vibrant flavors of Mexico to your kitchen.

We understand that in even the most well-oiled kitchens, a small mistake can occasionally slip through. However, we hope that you can see past these minor hiccups and focus on the passion we've invested in this cookbook.

With each recipe, we've aimed to create not just a dish but an experience. Your trust in our culinary guide is our greatest honor. Your connection to our recipes and the delightful dishes you've created with them have warmed our hearts.

We eagerly await the opportunity to embark on more culinary adventures with you, to explore the rich tapestry of Mexican cuisine, and to serve as your trusted companion in the kitchen. Your experiences inspire us to keep learning, growing, and innovating.

As we bid adieu to this colorful journey, we want to express our heartfelt thanks for choosing "Mexican Fiesta with 5 Ingredients" as your culinary companion. Your loyalty and love for Mexican cuisine provide the purpose and spice to our culinary voyage.

With profound appreciation and a shared love for Mexican fiesta,
**Garden of Grapes**